THE COLLEGE ESSAY

What Would Dracula Do?

A Comprehensive Guide in 5 Steps

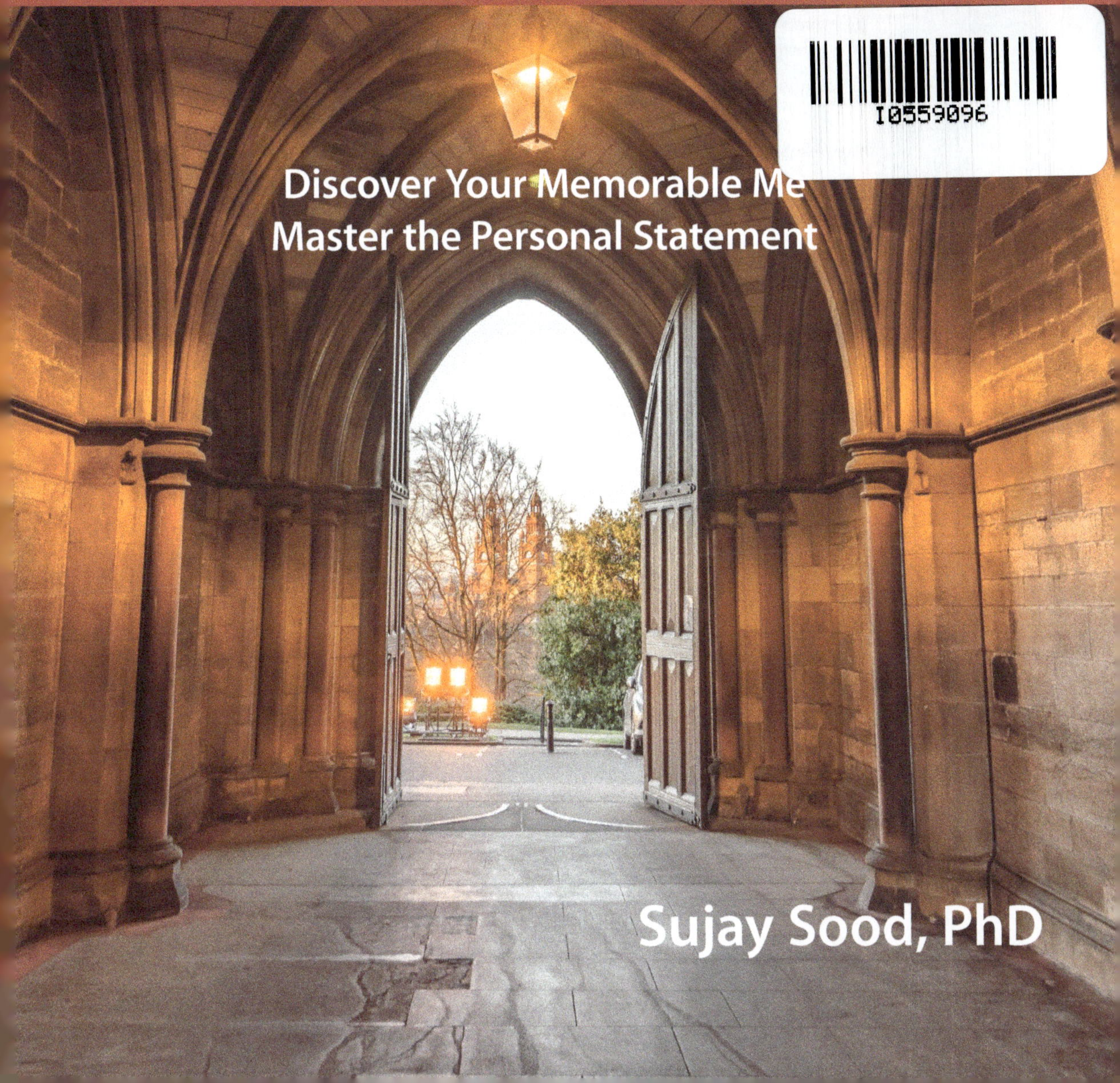

Discover Your Memorable Me
Master the Personal Statement

Sujay Sood, PhD

First Published August 2024
This edition published August 2024 by Essayt.com, LLC publishers
Great Neck, New York
www.essayt.com

Digital ISBN: 979-8-9911853-0-1
Paperback ISBN: 979-8-9911853-1-8
Hardcover ISBN: 979-8-9911853-2-5

Cover and text design by Michael O'Donnell.
Image credit: ©2023 KenSoftTH/Shutterstock.
Description: "Glasgow, UK March 27, 2023: Historic Cloisters of Glasgow University with light up illumination featuring classic scottish gothic architecture."

Visit www.essayt.com for any further information.

TABLE OF CONTENTS

Preface iv

How to Use This Book vi

A Note to You, the College Applicant vii

A Note to Teachers viii

Part 1: Applying to College 1

Introduction: The College Essay is Not an Essay 2

Chapter 1: Buna Ziua. My Name is Dracula 8

Chapter 2: What the College Application Needs 11

Part 2: Dracula's Essays: A Case Study 17

Chapter 3: Dracula Writes 7 Common App Essays 18

Chapter 4: Rejectionville 33

Chapter 5: Dracula Searches for College Essay Help 38

Chapter 6: Please Understand the Purpose, Dracula! 40

Part 3: What is Purposeful Writing? 50

Chapter 7: Your Turn: Identify the Errors in "Great Writing" 51

Chapter 8: What Dracula Got Wrong (and Right) 73

Chapter 9: Essential Elements of Style in Writing 98

Part 4: Find Your Memorable Me 114

Chapter 10: Find Your Memorable Me 115

Chapter 11: What About AI and GPTs? 133

Chapter 12: Dracula's Gems (Rewritten College Essays) 146

Appendix: The Memorable Me Worksheets 154

PREFACE

How do you find your voice and make it heard?

That's the question of the moment.

If you are here, it is because you want to write that winning college essay that will make a world of difference to your chances of gaining admission to the college of your dreams.

You don't want to write a yawner. In fact, **you want to be memorable.**

You don't want to be a stereotype. What you want to be is authentic.

The first thing to realize is that **you are not writing an essay.**

I'll say it again: you are not writing an essay.

The College Essay is not an essay.

For all intents and purposes, The College Essay is a story.

You are writing a compelling story about "Your Journey So Far."

And, since it is a story, just like every story you have read in your life, it needs a hero. A protagonist. Oh, and themes. Definitely themes. Remember all those English classes?

And guess what? you are it!

You are the hero of the journey of your life.

So all you need to do is craft a compelling narrative that highlights all the amazing adventures—and trials and tribulations—that have shaped you into the type of college candidate who makes the admissions officer exclaim, "Oh my god, I want this student to belong on my campus with all the other amazing students that are already frolicking here!"

And, you have to do this in 650 words or less.

How do you get this done and get this done well?

This book will guide you step by step to craft that winning story of "Your Journey So Far" also known as The College Essay.

In this book, I have distilled my knowledge and experience from over 25 years of workshopping, advising, and helping thousands of students to write the best possible version of themselves and get that all important edge on their application.

Do realize that The College Essay is crucial because it is the only component of your application packet that is 100% in your control. The rest—GPA, coursework, SAT and ACT scores, extracurriculars, teacher recommendations—is out of your hands.

The College Essay—which we will call "The Story of Your Journey So Far" is your opportunity to showcase:

- Your individuality
- Your personality
- Your uniqueness

In short, showcase **what makes you you** and **what makes you memorable?**

How will you persuade the admissions officer to give you that cherished spot over twenty or thirty other equally qualified candidates?

What are we waiting for? Let us begin!!

How to Use This Book

(The Best Way, The Quick Way, and The Desperate Way)

The Best Way to Get This Done

- Do not rush it
- Read it in more than a few sittings
- Absorb the "Did You Know" and "Pro Tip" inserts
- Enjoy Dracula's journey with the college application process
- Read Dracula's college essays
- Try to identify the shortcomings in Dracula's writing
- Fill out the prompts to identify errors
- Read Dr. Sood's critique of Dracula's essays
- Gain familiarity with the essential elements of style for college writing
- Follow Dracula as he does The College Essay worksheets
- Observe Dracula's guided interaction with Chat Gpt & Gemini AI
- Read the new and improved essay "gems" crafted by Dracula
- Complete the 5-Step worksheets
- Craft your own college essay "gem"

The Quick Way to Use This Book

- Absorb the "Did You Know" and "Pro Tip" inserts
- Read Dracula's college essays (Ch 3)
- Fill out the interactive prompts (Ch 7)
- Read Dr. Sood's critique of Dracula's essays (Ch 8)
- Gain familiarity with the essential elements of style for college writing (Ch 9)
- Follow Dracula as he does The College Essay worksheets (Ch 10)
- Complete the 5-step worksheets (Appendix)
- Observe Dracula's guided interaction with Chat Gpt & Gemini AI (Ch 11)
- Read the new and improved essay "gems" crafted by Dracula (Ch 12)
- Craft your own College Essay "gem"

The Desperate Way to Use This Book

- Absorb the "Did You Know" and "Pro Tip" inserts
- Follow Dracula as he does The College Essay worksheets (Ch 10)
- Complete the 5-step worksheets (Appendix)
- Gain familiarity with the essential elements of style for college writing (Ch 9)
- Observe Dracula's guided interaction with Chat Gpt & Gemini AI (Ch 11)
- Read Dracula's new and improved essays (Ch 12)
- Compose your own College Essay "gem"

A Note to You, the College Applicant

I believe in self-empowerment.

Having put in close to 30 years teaching at college and high school and having helped thousands of students with their personal statements, I can attest to two things: first, the college essay is its own beast and its importance surpasses anything you have ever written up until now; second, once you understand what the college essay is and what it needs, you realize that you have been shown all along how to write a great one.

That is, if you were paying attention in English class. If you were not, you might be misled into thinking that you will have to spend hundreds and maybe thousands on a college essay tutor or coach.

This book is going to empower you to write an amazing college essay yourself.

In this book, I have put together everything I taught for decades to students in the classroom—from understanding the purpose of the college essay, to recognizing the shortcomings of ostensibly well written essays, to workshopping your "Memorable Me" onto the page, to crafting that essential 650-word document that will take your college application to the next level.

And, even better, if you absorb all the skill and insights that this book offers into the writing process, then I can also assure you that you will become a confident writer equipped with the elements of style for great writing in college and beyond.

We live in the age of AI writing tools, and one of the chapters provides guided interaction with AI. Sure, AI will generate writing that sounds good if not great, but it is also writing that is a bit too uniform, a tad too repetitive, and much too lacking in personality.

AI writing has no authentic nor memorable me, but instead speaks with a generic monotone that proclaims, "A machine wrote this! A machine wrote this!"

So use this book well: absorb what it takes to become a great writer and use AI as a personal assistant as need be.

I wish you all the best in your journey.

A Note to Teachers

One can reformulate Tolstoy's famous opening from Anna Karenina to state, "All mediocre college essays are alike, each great college essay is great in its own way."

While there is no single recipe for The College Essay, the successful essay speaks from a place of authenticity, a place inhabited by a singular human being. And while the great college essay has attributes in both form and content that are recognizable and reproducible, each great essay tells its story with its own unique voice.

Drawing on my experience of teaching the ins and outs of what makes a successful college essay, I have put together a book that addresses all aspects of The College Essay writing process.

Today, "all aspects" requires a nod to the ubiquity of generative AI tools such as Chat Gpt and Gemini AI. It would be disingenuous to assume that high school students will not avail of these services, and it would be irresponsible to not provide some guidance on how to use this formidable yet limited tool. Given input shaped by the worksheets, AI will churn out portions of prose that could well set the writer down an original path; what it will do well is give unflagging attention to punctuation, grammar, and spelling.

More importantly, let me answer the question, "Why Dracula?" Or, "What has Dracula got to do with teaching how to write The College Essay?"

I envision one purpose for this book as a companion guide to the Bram Stoker's *Dracula*. Stoker's seminal tale is found on the curricula for junior and senior English classes, and the content in this book has been designed to enrich literary discussion and interpretation. The essays Count Dracula writes on his own are not only crafted in literary language but are also inspired by a deep dive into Bram Stoker's original sources.

Thus, a pairing of this book with Stoker's Dracula will invigorate class discussion but also segue nicely to teaching the essential components of The College Essay.

Another reason I have chosen to workshop The College Essay through Dracula's perspective is to show how even though the essay might sound great and though it might come from someone who has an abundance of experiences to draw upon, it could still fail to serve the purpose of this all important 650-word document.

Finally, who doesn't love Dracula?

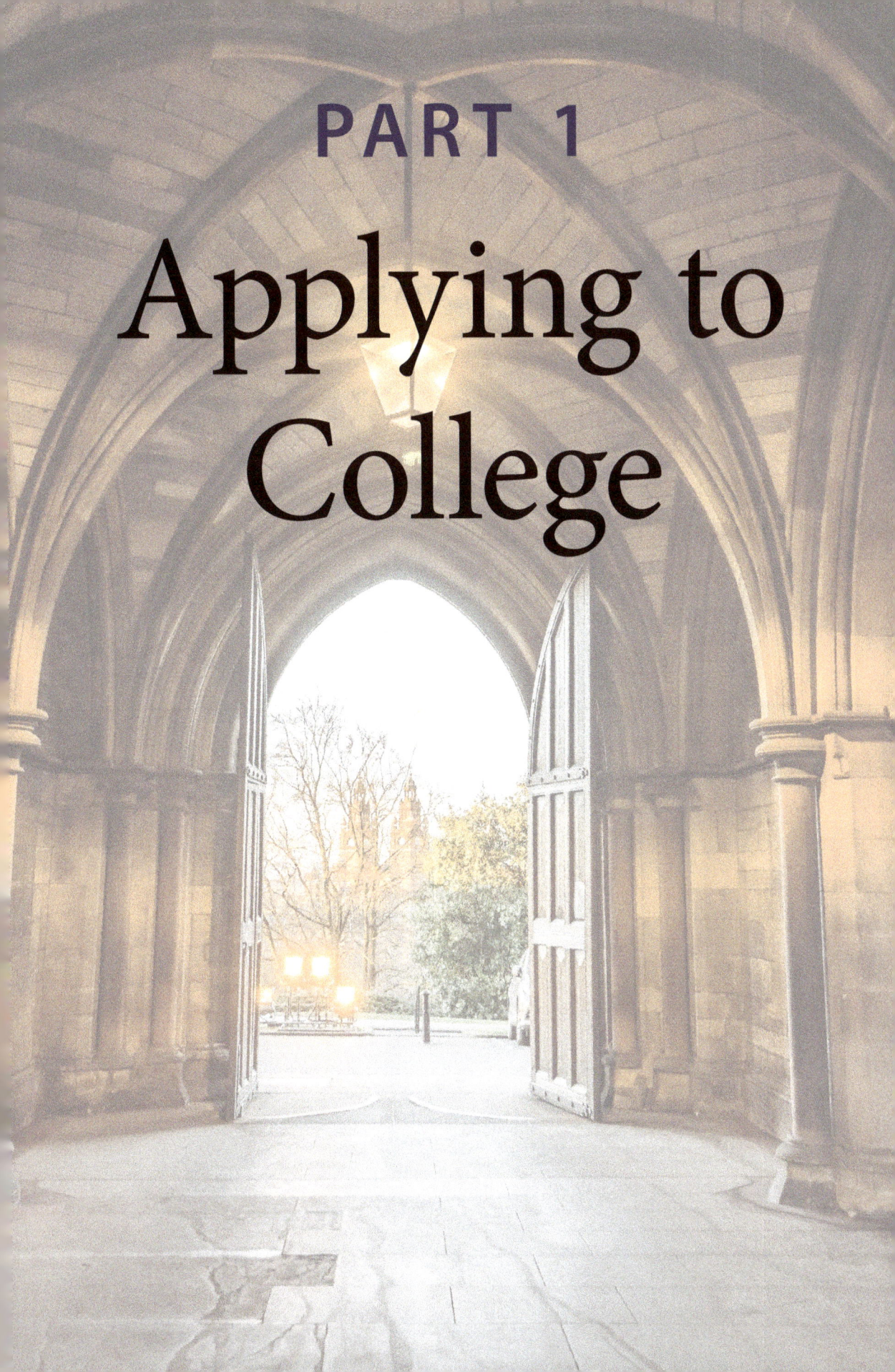

PART 1
Applying to College

INTRODUCTION
The College Essay is Not an Essay

A s you begin to understand what the so-called college essay is all about, you'll be asking the following question: "Why do they even call it "The College Essay" when it is not an essay?!"

And there lies the truth. This 650-word document, the most important 650 words of your young life, this so-called "College Essay" is not an essay at all but a story.

The College Essay is a story. **A story about you.**

And by now you have paid just about enough attention to English class to know: every story needs a hero. Or, more formally, a protagonist.

And guess what? You are it. You are the protagonist. **You are the hero.**

Wait a minute, you say—how exactly am I supposed to be the hero of anything? I am just a regular, high-school teenager who barely has time to look up from all my academics and extracurriculars.

Well, believe it or not, you have always been the hero of your own, unique and personal journey in life. Every move you make, every breath you take you are adding to your hero's journey—a journey full of trials and tribulations, successes and failures, the happiest of highs and lowest of lows, and pretty much everything else in between.

If you think about it, The College Essay (a story, not an essay) is actually a cool activity: it is an invitation for you to pause and take stock of the journey of your life so far in a manner that you have never done before.

As the hero of your journey, what amazing moments have you lived? What foundational experiences have been yours? What friends, what mentors, what guides have helped you along? And, who has been the most villainous of villains?

In short, you are going to discover the great story of you: how the hero in you has navigated your journey in life so far—a journey that has had its fair share of obstacles, challenges, and triumphs.

Let us take some common obstacles and challenges: low test score, difficulty with a subject, not making the team, getting benched, time management, late assignment, fitting in, broken friendship, unsympathetic teacher, family emergency, broken heart, dog ate homework—the list goes on.

And yet, you are strong. You are resilient. You are resourceful. You have done your best to overcome all setbacks. Hey, you have faced down puberty and won! You have grown from your experiences, you have learned your lessons, you have found ways to succeed.

Because basically, that is what a hero does—a hero overcomes obstacles in the journey of life and in doing so grows into a better person, the type of person that others look up to and admire.

The type of person that others want to be around.

The type of person that college admissions committees want on their campus.

Let us think about these college admissions committees for a quick second.

An admissions committee is made up of a bunch of well intentioned, well educated, yet highly overworked individuals. They're overwhelmed by their caseloads—hundreds of college applications by students such as yourself—and these admissions officers are working under many guidelines and criteria for choosing whose application is shortlisted and moved forward, and whose application gets crossed out and dumped onto the rejection pile.

And the reality of this situation is that the pile of shortlisted applications is tiny in comparison to the mountain of rejections.

So, how do you stand out?

 Pro Tip: Be sure each sentence in your college essay is about you: if what you're saying is also true for all your classmates, don't say it!

How do you end up in the shortlisted pile of applications?

Honestly, there is no silver bullet. But, there is the all important college essay also known as the personal statement also known as the story of your journey in life so far.

Follow the guidance in this book, and I give my assurance that you will craft a story that is going to be memorable and linger long after the reading is done.

Your story will jerk the admissions officer out of the somnolence that comes from reading application after application after application, and excite them enough to nudge another drowsy colleague to exclaim, "Hey, listen to the amazing story this student just shared…!"

Heroes are memorable.

It is time to discover what makes you a hero.

What Makes a Hero?

If you have been paying attention, then you might have thoughts along the lines of:

- *Wait…if that's true, then how am I supposed to write a story about myself that's going to stand out from the stories of all the other graduating seniors on the planet?*
- *How can I write a hero's story that's going to be unique, authentic, and memorable?*
- *I'm only seventeen, I haven't even lived my life yet! I'm just like everyone else…*

Take a deep breath. Relax. I am here to share good news.

Thanks to the brilliant research done by Joseph Campbell in the book *The Hero with a Thousand Faces*, we have a blueprint not only of what makes a hero but also an understanding of how the hero resides in each and everyone of us.

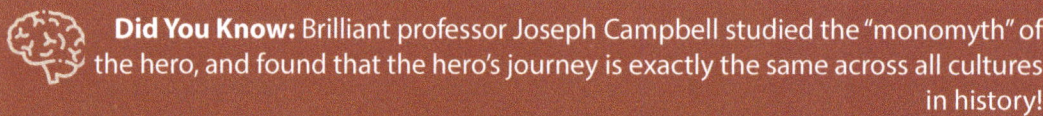

Did You Know: Brilliant professor Joseph Campbell studied the "monomyth" of the hero, and found that the hero's journey is exactly the same across all cultures in history!

You are probably familiar with the hero's journey map (see insert). Chances are your English teacher gave you this handout or something very similar to it in middle school or high school and asked you to map the protagonist's quest onto it.

The Hero's Journey aka Your Journey In Life

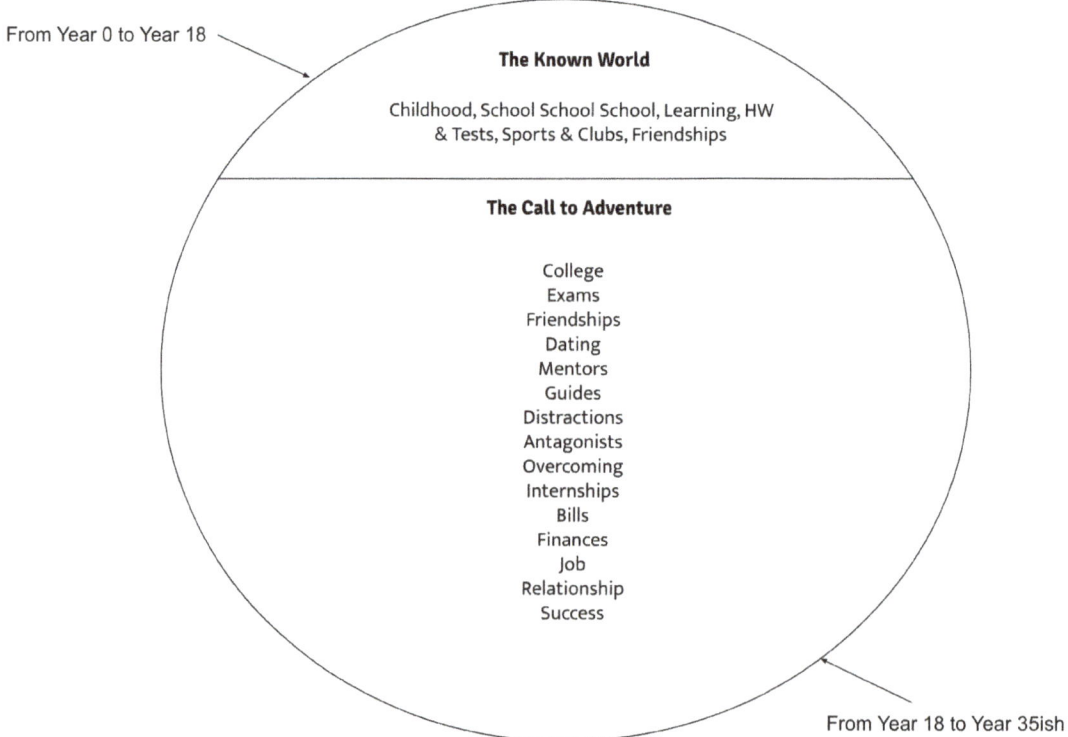

From Year 0 to Year 18

The Known World

Childhood, School School School, Learning, HW & Tests, Sports & Clubs, Friendships

The Call to Adventure

College
Exams
Friendships
Dating
Mentors
Guides
Distractions
Antagonists
Overcoming
Internships
Bills
Finances
Job
Relationship
Success

From Year 18 to Year 35ish

In a nutshell, our hero lives an ordinary life in an ordinary world. Then, something dramatic takes place to snatch our hero out of the everyday world and propel them into the unknown.

Here, the hero embarks on a quest full of adventure, finds a mentor, gains an ally, meets with deception, and ultimately does battle with the Shadow, the villain of the piece. And after facing the pit of despair, the hero overcomes—against all odds—and vanquishes the villain.

In doing so, the hero grows and transforms into someone worthy of admiration and respect. And upon returning home, the hero realizes they are completely different from their old self that set out on the quest.

You are soon going to leave home for college. Quite literally, you will be leaving the familiar, everyday world for adventures and obstacles of the unknown world of college and adulthood—a brand new hero's journey awaits!

So here's the secret: life is made up of a series of quests, big and small. The quest could be grammar, it could be math, it could be science; it could be trying to improve that backhand in tennis, run that lap faster on the track, swish that three-pointer on the court; it could be trying to mend a friendship, seek validation, gain approval; it could be trying to assert yourself in a group, become a better public speaker, or simply raise your hand in the classroom.

The narrative structure of the hero fits pretty much every story you can think of. Peter Parker? Check. Dorothy Gale in Kansas? Check. Harry Potter, Frodo Baggins, Catniss Everdeen? Check, check, and check.

You? Check.

But of course, this structure goes all the way back to when stories were first written and heroes were first invented.

Odysseus, Gilgamesh, and Rama but also Jesus, Buddha, and Mohammed.

But just like in the case of the chicken or the egg, one might ask what comes first—the hero or the story of the hero's journey?

Mythological or religious, historical or fictional, big or small—Campbell argues that one thing all heroes share in common is that they tap into a higher purpose, a deeper meaning, and a universal source. This experience is transformative and its proof is in the recognition afforded by others in society: the hero never needs to announce themself.

The hero is readily recognizable by all.

How do I get this done?

You are thinking, *I get it. The College Essay is not an essay. It is a story about me. I'm the hero. So like, where do I begin?*

Easy: take a notepad and pen, and begin to jot down all those occasions when you faced an obstacle and ultimately triumphed. Be sure to include all those experiences that helped you grow, and all those obstacles that you overcame, and explain how you began to transform into a hero with a new set of skills and a fresh perspective on life.

And now you are likely thinking:

- *How in the name of all that is sacred and holy will I ever be able to convey all this in 650 words or less?!*
- *How do I know what experiences will make me memorable to the admissions committee?*
- *How can I convey the formidable candidate that I am in just 650 words?*

Fear not. You have come to the right place.

I have been helping college candidates such as yourself for decades. Each and everyone that I have worked with has walked away with a memorable story of **My Journey In Life So Far.**

In a nod to anti-ageism, I must confess that plenty of college applicants aren't your typical teenager-fresh-out-of-high-school. Some of the most interesting college candidates I have helped over the past few years have been older—in their 20's, 30's, and even 40's—but the questions they have asked and the advice they have sought have basically been indistinguishable from those asked by the high schoolers:

- *How do I write a great college essay?*
- *What are they looking for?*
- *How will I make myself stand out?*

 Did You Know: Aristotle, the father of Rhetoric, pointed out that the art of persuasion needs three appeals working in tandem: emotional force, logical force, and ethical force.

In the following pages, you'll find a step by step guide that'll take you from zero to hero.

And hey, the process outlined in these pages helped no less than the great Count Dracula to highlight aspects of his nefarious journey and craft memorable college essays of his own.

Count Dracula and The College Essay

Yes, you read that right. Count Dracula. The Prince of Darkness. The granddaddy of vampires. The original undead applying to college and banging out college essays.

This has got to be a joke! is what I thought when the gentleman in question first queried me for college essay writing advice. A clever gimmick, no doubt, from a college candidate who wants to present himself as the eponymous count of the fantastical vampire legend. What a clever way to stand out! What a unique concept to be memorable!

Imagine my shock upon our first meeting when the client who showed up was none other than the Count Dracula that lurks deep within the recesses of our collective unconscious. The more we talked, the more convinced I became that the man before me was none other than the original item, the deathless and undying Count from Transylvania.

Imagine my greater shock upon learning that Count Dracula was not seeking to chomp down on my jugular vein but instead seeking my counsel with the college application in general and The College Essay in particular.

To top it off, the Count had come to me not because he was applying for college but because he had been *rejected* from all colleges he had already applied to!

Yes, Count Dracula had suffered what countless young mortals suffer every year: rejection after rejection after rejection from colleges.

How was this possible?!

 Pro Tip: Do not waste time regurgitating stuff they already know from your application packet such as grades, resume, clubs—tell them what they don't yet know about you!

If he indeed were Count Dracula, he was unique, special, and memorable even before he needed to part his lips to reveal those razor sharp predatory canines.

How could Count Dracula end up getting rejected from all the colleges he had applied to? What did he do wrong? Could I even be of assistance? Well, dear reader, I have recorded in as straightforward a manner as possible the details of my work with the most unusual client ever. I share the same with you holding the belief that the insights into The College Essay writing process will benefit you in your quest for admissions as much as they did Count Dracula.

CHAPTER 1
Buna Ziua. My Name is Dracula

Buna ziua. Hello. My name is Dracula. You might have heard of my story, how I broadened my horizons and gained awareness of a different culture when I traveled from my homeland of Transylvania to London, England in the late 1800s.

I learned a lot!

But now that I'm hunting in America, I have decided to apply to college. An American college. Everybody wants to study in the United States, myself included. Yes, me—Count Dracula!

I'm dying to be a freshman, dying to live in a dorm, dying to party with young blood. What better place for fresh meat!

If you have heard of me, which you most certainly have, you know that my case is special: I never age. But that is only the physical part of me, because I do grow and I do mature.

A good body is nothing without a good mind. My mind is ever curious and ever open to knowledge. In the journey of life, through all the roads I have taken and in all the vampire converts I have shall we say kissed, I have always chosen the toughest of challenges.

What comes easy is forgettable. What comes with sacrifice is delectable.

The harder the journey, the tastier the dish at its end.

I have an insatiable appetite—for learning as much as for some of the other things we don't need to rehash here. The point is, if you are not constantly learning, feeding, and transforming then life will leave you behind.

In the research I've done regarding the college application process, I've come across a bunch of buzzwords that everyone thinks are essential to showcase, and you'll allow me the slightest of wolfish grins as I proclaim that it is clear that no candidate in the history of college applications is going to be more qualified than yours truly, Count Dracula. Indeed, I am:

- Passionate
- Well-rounded
- Interdisciplinary
- Unique
- Underrepresented

 Did You Know: Your task is to excite the admissions officer into wanting you to intermingle with all the other young adults on their campus.

Or, let us use three words to describe my personality: Incisive. Penetrating. Piercing.

Most of all: Transformative.

I hear colleges hate static candidates but love dynamic ones, those who are willing and open to change. I, Count Dracula, can pretty much change into anything I want. Wolf, bat, vapor, sparkling dust, you name it.

But now I need to change into the vampire with the vogue, the nightwalker in the know. The reason being that your world, human, has changed so incredibly much from the one I was familiar with through centuries of my night prowl that I hardly recognize it.

Speaking of recognition, no one in the streets of Manhattan seems to recognize me these days. I walk in plain sight and flash my seductive, shall we say wolfish, smile at one and all. I am tall, debonair, and well-dressed. Some might even say charming. Yet, that dropdead smile I perfected through the centuries goes unnoticed.

No one looks up long enough in today's smartphone obsessed world.

And when they do see me, they think I'm an extra from a Broadway Show at best to a caricature hired to promote a product at worst. I'm dressed the same as I always was for centuries in Europe. Bespoke tailoring to convey elegance and refinement, a cane to conceal the razor blade I might never need, and a top hat to confer respect to my prey.

But people today mistake what I wear for a costume. Come on, folks—it's me, Count Dracula, the real slim shady, not some sorry Halloween wannabe. (My favorite holiday, by the way—what a day for feasting!)

Now that I've lived here long enough, though, I'm starting to resent all the cultural appropriation rampant in this day and age. I'm going to write a book on it after I graduate, *Everything But The Blood—What Americans are taking from Vampire Culture.*

First things first. I must get admitted into a great college.

Back in my day, you didn't have to get a degree to learn something, you just learned by doing. You worked with someone who knew the trade, you became their apprentice, and one day you became the master of your craft. Butcher, coroner, coffin-maker, embalmer— possibilities galore.

Today, if you ever want to get taken seriously, you have to prove that you went to some big name school and took a series of liberal arts courses while actually majoring in some #trendy STEM subject.

Imagine if back in the day, they had forced me to attend blood-transfusion school. Or canine-implant school. Or shape-shifting school. *Phah!* In those days, you learned by sinking your teeth into the subject.

But today, without that college degree, you are nothing.

And, you can't just talk your way into the equivalent of brandishing a college degree no matter how much real-life knowledge and experience you might have.

"Hi, I'm Count Dracula and I have a Ph.D. of the night" won't cut it anywhere.

"Where did you go to undergrad?" They'll ask.

Well, I'm nothing if not proactive. As they say in the wolf friendly Carpathian mountains, if the blood doesn't come to you, you sniff out the blood. *Owooooo!*

CHAPTER 2
What the College Application Needs

Before I go any further, let me give a shout out to the Internet. What a boon! What a gift! Everything you could possibly want to know is on the internet. Fantastisch! It is a treasure trove of information and knowledge.

It is also full of crap, Seriously.

The Internet's got an unbelievable amount of junk. Take the stuff about me, Count Dracula. I never forgot anything I learned when I became the Undead. To think that I transformed—nay, ascended—to my vampiric existence equipped but with the mind of a child! An infamous conjecture popularized by a certain Dr. Van Helsing.

On the flip side, where would my college application be without the internet? Every academic institution is online. Every last detail of the application is listed for each college, and it turns out that the set of expectations is identical.

As far as I can tell, here's what I need to get into pretty much any college in the country:

- High school transcript
- Advanced coursework
- SAT/ACT scores
- Resume/extracurriculars
- Teacher recommendations
- The College Essay/personal statement

High School Transcript

About that. Should I send in the manuscript from 1167 AD attesting to my superior knowledge of sacral texts while I sampled the blood of monks at the Benedictine High School of Pannonhalma? Or should I send in a record of all the scriptures I transcribed while frolicking with 16th-century nuns at Einsiedeln Abbey in Switzerland? Would those impress an admissions committee more than the record I have from my days of carnal cavorting with the Bloomsbury Group at Cambridge in England?

Regardless of which document I choose, I'll be shelling out for an attested certification.

Not that I'm complaining, but it sure seems like this college application business is a money making scam.

Advanced Coursework

Where do I even begin? I have centuries worth of knowledge through self-study and apprenticeships. I can honestly say that from the beginning of my existence to about the 1850s, there was no branch of knowledge that I had not examined, ingested, and digested. Alchemy, necromancy, demonology, thaumaturgy, oneiromancy—I could have written the book on these and more.

But I'm faced with two problems: first, none of my favorite subjects seems to be #trending these days; second, showcasing myself as a know-it-all probably won't get me into the college of my dreams.

I don't know what happened to humans after the 1850's but their knowledge increased exponentially both in breadth and depth. (Human self-awareness has decreased in equal proportion, but that's a tale for another moonless night.)

So that now, believe it or not, I Count Dracula have gaps in knowledge akin to the rest of the pitiful mortals that comprise the human race. But there is good news: there are so many avenues of specialization that the menu of options makes me giddy with joy.

Why?

Because being undead, I have all the time in the world.

There is so much more I want to devour, knowledge included.

That is why I want to be a college freshman.

SAT/ACT Score

Yeah, okay—I see you, standardized test.

(Did I mention money-making scam? If every graduating high schooler needs it as part of their college application, then why isn't it free: administered by the government and paid for by tax dollars?)

Resume

As you might imagine, my resume could go on for pages. But as they say in America, I need to cut to the chase. Keep it short: one-pager, please!

Count Dracula

Vampire at large

Skills

Experience

Education

Awards

Count Dracula
Scary Castle of Gloom & Doom
Borgo Pass, Carpathian Mountains
Transylvania, Romania

+40 123.LUV.BLUD
CountDracula@essayt.com

---

shape -shifting, predatory prowess, hypnotism, possession, blood work, soul-enslavement, infinite charm, longevity, seduction, resourcefulness, evasion, flight, swordplay, archery & crossbow, MMA

The Undead Corps / CEO & General Manager
JANUARY 1377 - PRESENT, GLOBAL ENTERPRISE

Implement strategy to maintain 100% retention rates of all personnel. Execute an International Expansion Strategy which saw 38% increase in conversion. Streamline supply chains of essential fodder. Communicate physically with high-level converts to create everlasting blood bonds.

Gloom & Doom Realty / Property Manager
JANUARY 1377 - PRESENT, GLOBAL ENTERPRISE

Stock all acquired properties with native soil and sufficient coffins for residents. Maintain 100% occupancy rate during feeding season. Utilize Airbnb, VRBO, and HomeAway for initial infiltration of new territories. Process credit checks for potential residents. Investigate and resolve tenant complaints. Foster codependency and blood addiction

Dracul Capital Partners / Chief Investment Banker
JANUARY 20XX - MONTH 20XX, WALL STREET, NEW YORK

Implement due diligence investigation of new assets, leverage the Firm to foster a strong culture of acquiescence from donors, maintain the ledger for the range of Undead vassals, participate in industry conferences to create a bite-list for prospective clients/vassals

---

Count Dracula High School/ High School Diploma
SEPTEMBER 2018 - JUNE 2022, www.cdhs.bite

A range of high level courses in the arts and sciences, achieve a 5 score on all APs administered by the College Board, audit online courses at Khan Academy, certification from Harvard University's Free Online Courses (JavaScript, AI)

Order of the Lorem ipsum, Knight Templar of the Consectetur, Purple Heart of the French Legion, Order of Valor Montenegro

Having researched the nuts and bolts of an effective resume, I've found that the High School Resume is an animal of its own, tailored to embellishing the modest accomplishments of teenagers.

After several edits, I've come up with a winning high school resume. "Look on it and weep, ye mortals!" as my friend Ozymandias was fond of saying between my bloodsuck nibbles.

Recommendations

This part seems straightforward enough. Ask someone who knows you in an academic or professional capacity to write a letter of wholehearted praise.

 Pro Tip: In Your Junior year, target two teachers for recommendations. Participate in their class, help them when you can, visit them during office hours.

As you might expect, over the centuries I have bloodsucked countless luminaries into my way of existence.

I have a legion of vassals in my service, ranging from world leaders, Nobel laureates, innovators, and humanitarians.

I, Count Dracula, am the original influencer.

So, what kind of recommender should I select to vouch for my wondrous vampirical valiance? Clearly, I need to answer the following questions before I create a short list of recommenders:

What combination of recommenders will be most effective?

Who not only knows me intimately but also can convey my superlative qualities in writing?

Who is still not only undead but also sane?

 Pro Tip: The brag sheet is as much for your teachers as it is for you. Be sure to brag about your highlights in that teacher's class, making their job of recommending you as easy as can be.

Once I have a shortlist, I have to provide them with a brag sheet of my accomplishments so that they can be expedient in composing that winning recommendation letter.

It would also be useful to have one recommendation from an Alumni for each school I apply to: Harvard alum for Harvard app, Stanford Alum for Stanford App, Cal Tech Alum for CalTech app, and so on and so forth.

The only problem I foresee with this recommendation business is the tediousness of it all. Keep track of whom I ask, who responds, who commits, who needs additional information, who submits online, who submits snail mail, who needs a nudge for approaching deadlines, who needs to be thanked.

And, who deserves a friendly reminder with a visitation in the dead of night.

> **Pro Tip:** Keep a spreadsheet to keep track of your applications. Column headers: Colleges applied to, deadlines, requirements, recommendations, recommender names, and finally, an "application complete" column.

But this, my friend, is why they invented spreadsheets.

The College Essay

Last but not least, The College Essay. The final component of an application dossier.

I have it on good authority that when all else is equal—GPA & transcript, strength of course work, recommendations, resume, extra-curriculars—then this little 650 word document showcasing who you are becomes all important.

I first wondered how many different essays I would have to write and if that maybe would limit my college applications.

> **Pro Tip:** One great college essay is all you need. On the Common Application, prompt 7 is open-ended: you can write about anything. Once you have a gem, you adapt it for each college as need be.

But have no fear! There is something called the Common Application. One, yes one application for 900 plus schools! it is bloody perfect! To top it off, they provide you seven essay prompts and you respond to only one. Easy peasy!

One-size-fits all option *à la Americaine!* (Did I mention I love America?!)

Let us see here...

1. Some students have a background, identity, interest, or talent that is so meaningful they believe their application would be incomplete without it. If this sounds like you, then please share your story.

2. The lessons we take from obstacles we encounter can be fundamental to later success. Recount a time when you faced a challenge, setback, or failure. How did it affect you, and what did you learn from the experience?

3. Reflect on a time when you questioned or challenged a belief or idea. What prompted your thinking? What was the outcome?

4. Reflect on something that someone has done for you that has made you happy or thankful in a surprising way. How has this gratitude affected or motivated you?

5. Discuss an accomplishment, event, or realization that sparked a period of personal growth and a new understanding of yourself or others.

6. Describe a topic, idea, or concept you find so engaging that it makes you lose all track of time. Why does it captivate you? What or who do you turn to when you want to learn more?

7. Share an essay on any topic of your choice. It can be one you've already written, one that responds to a different prompt, or one of your own design.

Did You Know: The landmark Supreme Court ruling in 2023 ended affirmative action in higher education? If you have a significant racial background, be sure to embed it in the Story Of Your Journey So Far.

I am Count Dracula. 650 words or less. Piece of cake. Where do I begin?

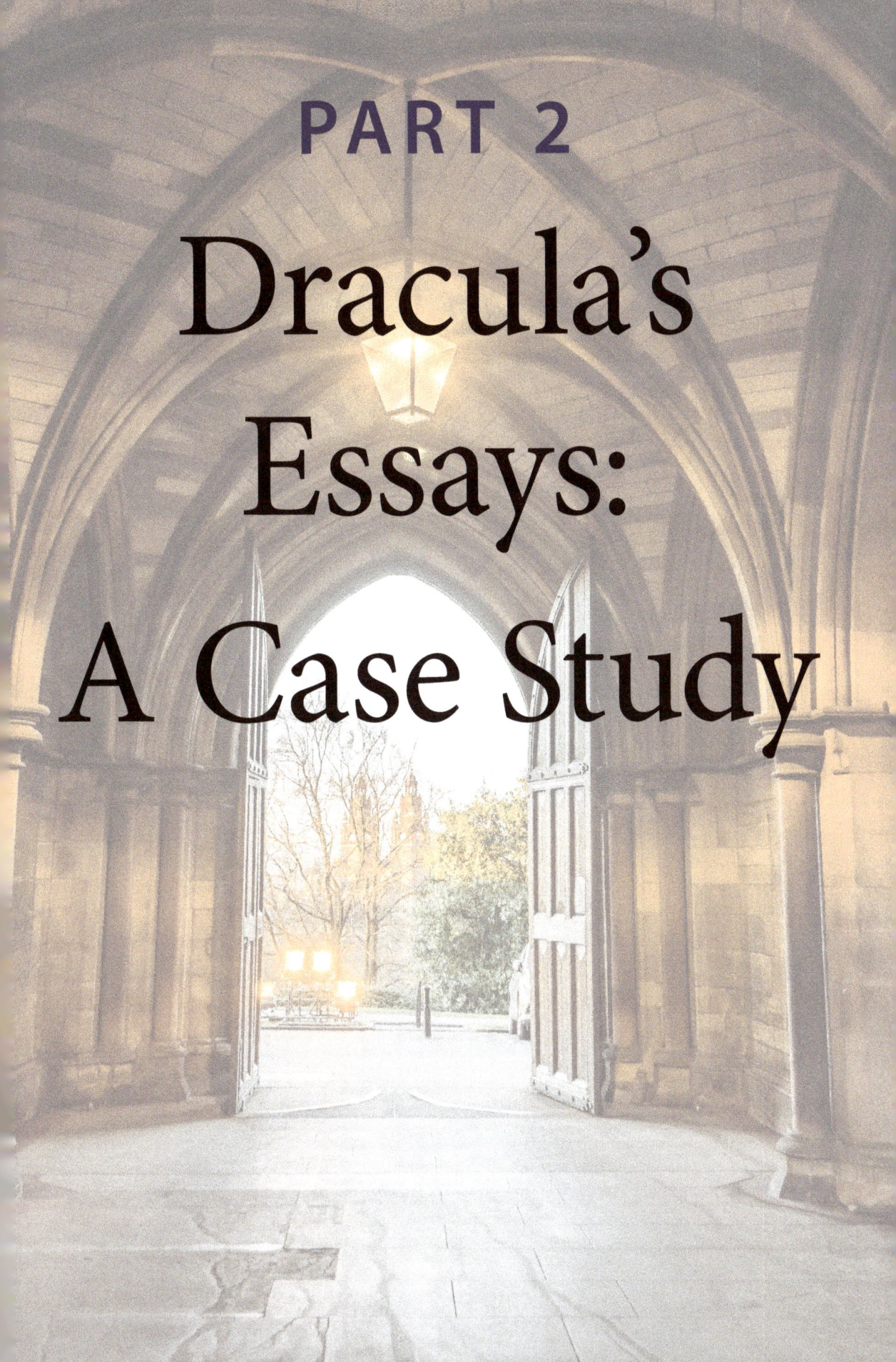

PART 2

Dracula's Essays:

A Case Study

CHAPTER 3
Dracula Writes 7 Common App Essays

1. **Some students have a background, identity, interest, or talent that is so meaningful that their application would be incomplete without it. If this sounds like you, then please share your story.**

(Were they thinking of me, Count Dracula, when they created this prompt? I am unique in each of these categories: my background, my identity, my interest, my talent! Quite obviously my application would be incomplete without it.)

Here goes:

Unlike mere mortals, my consciousness doesn't begin at birth. I have always been Count Dracula. I am not of mother born nor of father seeded. My existence knows neither childhood nor aging. I am extra-racial but not extra-terrestrial (at least not to my knowledge). Popular culture considers me to be Carpathian or Romanian, Szekelian or Hungarian, Dacian or Thracian—but, I ask you, can you truly pigeonhole the ethnicity of a shape-shifting, form-changing, mutant-morphing creature of the night such as myself? I don't think so.

Which brings me to my unique identity. I am the original vampire. While my condition has been seen as an affliction or disease or some grievous wrong against the natural order of being, I can assure you that I live and breathe with the same purpose my acolyte Darwin recognized more than a century ago: survival and procreation. Though in my superhuman adaptability, the propagation of my species (vampires) is advanced biology.

Yes, I am a lover and make love but not sex. It is the bite—the transfusion and transmission—that creates my progeny.

I never give birth, but I rebirth humans into my likeness of being.

The selection of which human to elevate into my higher plane of existence relies on my innate talent of being able to penetrate all defenses that suppress true desire. Not everyone desires the exhilaration of vampiric existence. Not everyone is worthy of such elevation.

But those that desire me and desire what I offer wonder, "How will I ever know if I am worthy of Count Dracula's bite? And how in Satan's name will Dracula be able to find me?"

Well, fear not, needy little homo sapien. My true talent, nay gift, is magnetic attraction to your innermost, deepest and darkest desires. Desires you know you have, desires you are ashamed to have, and desires you didn't know you had.

But I, Count Dracula, know your darkest desires! I feel them! I am drawn to them! It is your desire I feast on as I suck your blood! And if the rapture of our commingling is worthy enough, you are in! You are transfigured into my likeness and join my legion.

In all honesty, I consider this talent to be my greatest gift.

(375 words...too short. I don't know what else to write.)

2. The lessons we take from obstacles we encounter can be fundamental to later success. Recount a time when you faced a challenge, setback, or failure. How did it affect you, and what did you learn from the experience?

From the countless campaigns I waged over the centuries—as King and Commander in the Dark Ages, as Count and C.E.O in the Modern Ages—the setback that makes me most rueful is a fleeting episode in the saga of my somnambulist conquests. In England, in 1899, I identified nothing less than a woman worthy of ascension to Queen of the Undead. Her name was Mina Harker. Her pent up desires overwhelmed me with their unabashed embrace of the forbidden.

My very first glimpse of Mina, and I realized why London had been calling me all along, why I had endured passage in choppy seas, why I had acquired properties all across that grimy city, and why I had been putting myself out of my comfort zone by sleeping in rudimentary boxes filled with my native soil. Here she was, my wondrous Wilhelmina, kin of my kin, yearning for the liberation that only my teeth sunk deep into her neck could deliver.

But to get to Mina, to indoctrinate and to assimilate Mina, to absorb Mina and to transform her into becoming the queen of my coterie of undead countesses proved to be an abject failure.

My objectives were constantly thwarted by a bunch of do-gooders led by the nefarious Dr. Van Helsing, the luckiest devil to ever have crossed my path and survived. At me he thrust garlic, at me he brandished the Cross, at me he tossed sacramental wafers. And guess what? Because he found me repulsed, he thought his religion had power over me!

If only Helsing knew that I was affected not by any mystical force of his moronic charms but because of allergens! Brandish me your crucifix today, Van Helsing, and I'll brandish you my Epipen.

But I digress. Truth be told, even today I tip my hat to the resolve of the Helsing gang for making that concerted effort that thwarted my conquest of Mina.

They burst upon me during that primal moment when I had Mina entranced, ensconced in my bosom, and suckling the very life blood from the freshly incised artery in my chest. I was in a rapture, a delight swelling up in me that would surely explode to fill up the universe itself.

Mina had succumbed, her barriers had dissipated, and she was eager to merge. Perhaps I let my guard down and lingered too long in the bliss of this Vampire baptism. Perhaps I fell prey to my own overconfidence, but I failed to hear them until it was too late.

To my dismay, they were armed with all of the aforementioned allergens that debilitate me. I got so furious at the interruption of my bodacious banquet that I couldn't think straight and barely curbed my involuntary reaction of pouncing on the gang to tear them to shreds.

But sanity prevailed and I made my exit. At the time, I was rather sanguine about finding Mina and having her all to myself in the near future.

How wrong was I!

They worked in concert to infiltrate and booby trap all my coffin-boxes around London—in Carfax, Bermondsey, Mile End, Walworth. The men even had the temerity to lay an ambush for me at my abode in Piccadilly, armed as always with those god-forsaken allergens hidden in their crucifixes and wafers. Long story short, I was chased out of London and stalked all the way to my home in Transylvania. And Mina, I was never able to deliver the poor soul from her mortal existence, never able to give her what she truly desired—becoming Queen of the Undead and ruling by my side.

This failure affected me deeply. Despite my superior being, I was thwarted by mere mortals. I took the defeat to heart (no pun intended) and conducted a clinical analysis of why I had failed in my conquest of Mina and, more importantly, how I would never fail again in my future endeavors.

After much reflection, I realized that my enterprise suffered from inadequate preparation, planning, and execution in four domains: delegation, anticipation, underestimation and, last but not least, medication.

Delegation. I had gone solo. Never again. Granted, I am invincible; yet, I cannot be at multiple places at once. When faced by an enemy united in their numbers and coordinated in their actions, I cannot outmaneuver them by myself. For my expedition to London, I should have conscripted the services of the Three Sisters instead of leaving them behind to toy with Jonathan Harker. I should have used that profligate lunatic Renfield to greater advantage instead of too soon snapping his neck. I should have created my own little army of progeny to command and marshall in the field, disposing of them once they had performed their duties.

Anticipation. Sure, I was strategic in my plans, from the purchase of properties in prime locations, to shipping more than adequate supplies of native-soil coffins, to preying on my chosen women at the most opportune times. However, I paid scant regard to the possibility that my foes, though weaklings in most regards, were equally endowed with strategic acumen. While they anticipated my every move, I failed to examine their countermoves—they were playing chess not checkers. It was a humbling realization. From that moment forward, I always put myself in my adversaries' shoes before deciding on my next course of action.

Underestimation. I believed my adversary, the Helsing gang, to be weak just because they seemed to rely too much on religious icons. I was too quick to peg them with the religious fanatics I'd been encountering for centuries, people wed to superstition and dying for divine intervention. But Drs. Van Helsing, Seward et al. turned out to be confounding creatures whose swiftness for scientific experimentation was instrumental in defeating me. They figured out that the soil in my coffin had nutrients essential to my regeneration. They almost saved Lucy by administering blood transfusions. They collated multiple records of their interactions with me in order to analyze my predatory habits and create plans based on cold, hard logic. They exploited my telepathic bond with Mina. Underestimating their scientific acumen cost me victory. After London, I resolved: Never again.

Medication. if only they'd invented the epipen in 1899 instead of 1987. I go nowhere without it now. Come at me, crucifix! Whatchoo got, garlic?! Watch out, wafers! I have privately funded the development of multidose autoinjectors and I never leave home without it. You could say that the epipen is the only gun I'll ever need to carry into a battle and Epinephrine is my silver bullet. Whose street? My street!

(1107 words! Too long. I don't know what to cut...)

3. Reflect on a time when you questioned or challenged a belief or idea. What prompted your thinking? What was the outcome?

From the very onset of my existence, I have challenged the notion of binary sex and sexuality. Mine is a creative biology that literally transforms the site of desire from the conventional erogenous zones (genitalia, for most of you mortals) to those twin orifices on the neck: delicious, blood-tinged, and pulsing for more.

The world regards my conquests as victims, but they could not be more wrong! Properly speaking, both my "victim" and I are submissive partners, submitting to each other in turns. The blood I drink from your neck, the blood you drink from my bosom—a cycle of orgiastic becoming.

In my lovemaking, I am always subverting the heterodoxy of sexuality, turning on its head the belief system that males are males and females are females. I am the sole progenitor, I am both mother and father, father and mother, both husband and wife, and wife and husband. All my hordes are procreated from me and me alone.

People believe that bloodlust is what makes us vampires. They couldn't be further from the truth. What makes us vampires is the act of disrobing the garments imposed by society. Humans tend to wear the clothes chosen for them from the time of birth to the time of death: male to be blue to be boy, female to be pink to be girl.

To be vampire is to be black to be more.

To be vampire is to be a being without binary.

I wouldn't stir up a fuss about this except for the fuss stirred up by your kind, the males amongst the mortals. So much effort is expended in all parts of the world to hide the fact that the limitations of the roles males can play—and the roles females cannot play—is based on nothing more than arbitrary destiny.

One might say that I have chafed at this global conspiracy to keep men up and women down, and for centuries I have played the role of liberator, turning women to my cause.

I submit, with a sense of understated humility, that I, Count Dracula, am the first feminist.

So the question becomes: what has been the outcome of my concerted efforts at undermining and exposing male complicity in the global oppression of all others?

Clearly, I have been demonized by the male world. Theirs has been an unflagging smear-campaign fueled by the deep seated resentment of (male) power brokers around the planet. Their world might be divided in its representations of the devil as a tempting and sinful agent, but it is united in its portrayal of Dracula as a malevolent and unnatural beast.

Yet, there has been another outcome, a transformative change in society for which I am responsible but for which I will forever remain its unsung hero. I speak of the inexorable shift away from the oppression of patriarchy through the centuries.

Were it not for my late night jaunts across the world and into the bedchambers of the powerful, the world would not be in the state of gender liberation that it is today. The amount of research, planning, and execution I have undertaken in terms of identifying the best placed victims for vampiric conversion merits a Nobel Prize in Physiology or Medicine, perhaps even in Economics.

I have taken the best of the best females to the next level of biology and reduced the most vainglorious of men to compliance.

So many wars have I averted by a pointed nibble, simple possession and quick conversion of the right person at the right place and the right time.

This makes me wonder: why not the Nobel Peace Prize for Count Dracula?

(592 words. Getting there!)

4. Reflect on something that someone has done for you that has made you happy or thankful in a surprising way. How has this gratitude affected or motivated you?

Lucy Westenra.

If I might be allowed to claim that Mina Harker was my first experience of love at first sight, then I would like to aver that meeting Lucy in her unguarded somnambulance surprised me with a happiness I hadn't thought possible.

I will never cease to be grateful for what snowy Lucy in her white nightdress gave me that night in the ruins of St. Mary's Church. Little did I know as I lurked behind her bench watching the rays of the full moon slide down her exposed skin, that it was I who was about to be ravished.

What Lucy gave to me was the realization that there is always something new and unknown waiting to be discovered no matter how jaded by immortality you might be. Excuse me—how jaded by immortality I might be.

After all, when you have lived as long as I have, you have pretty much done it all, experienced it all. Believe it or not, being eternal has its drawbacks—not least of which is the fact that one is hard pressed to find any truly new, undiscovered, and unexpected pleasure in this monotony called the walking dead.

For how long had I been yearning to be yanked from the repetition of the same, and how unexpected was finding a novel intoxication in Lucy's embrace.

Simply put: I had never clasped any of my tender targets, never first sunk my eager canines into the soft curve of exposed neck whilst they were in that mysterious state of simultaneous consciousness and unconsciousness: the sleepwalker's drift.

You see, I had no idea that Lucy was in sleepwalking condition when she arched her back, stretched out her arms to clasp me by the neck, and drew me down from behind the bench for my first taste of her.

And how unexpectedly explosive the experience was! All the frustrations of my seaborne journey on that cursed ship *Demeter*, all the tension of my novel venture in that undiscovered country called England, all my perpetual watchful wariness of being a stranger in a strange land—all of it dissolved into an ecstasy of unbidden fireworks to rival the merriment of the dancing stars in the night sky above us. I became a mindless, powerless entity as her blood pulsed in my mouth, losing all reserve and all caution, wanting this moment to last forever, wanting to howl at the moon for eternity.

And how full of delight was the process of somnambulist conversion! Heretofore, I had been using the mesmeric power of my glowing eyes to entrance my victims, to make them swoon with unbidden desire for my suck. But Lucy's blood, as it pulsed its way down my throat, had me entranced with a whole host of sensations I hadn't known existed. The ecstasy was beyond belief. I lost all sense of time and space. I was floating in pure delight.

Only to be interrupted by Mina Harker!

Despite my raging fury at the untimely disruption, I held back from attacking Mina. Because, you see, I was working out how to relive my titillating tryst with Lucy. Ah, dear admissions committee, I wanted Lucy again and again and again. She had become my dependency.

The only question I kept asking myself was: how to prolong my carnal cavort with sleepwalking Lucy without completely converting her into a vampire?

Well, fortune was on my side. It was my very enemies led by Van Helsing who unwittingly ensured that Lucy would be replenished after our trysts to sleepwalk yet another night! In their zeal to revive her, they daily administered blood transfusions not knowing that they were merely replenishing her for our nighttime affairs.

And yet, all things human come to end. When Lucy crossed over and even before she was executed in cold blood by the Helsing group, I made a solemn promise: to do everything in my power to research the science behind somnambulist conversion.

For this unexpected and novel ecstasy, I will forever be grateful to you, my sweet sleepwalking Lucy.

(670 words. Practice makes perfect!)

5. Discuss an accomplishment, event, or realization that sparked a period of personal growth and a new understanding of yourself or others.

Albert, one of my favorite conversions, is often quoted for saying something that I personally told him when regaling him with tales from my days at the Scholomance in Romania. "Great spirits have always encountered violent opposition from mediocre minds." I came up with that quote first—you can ask him yourself if you find him, but he'll probably tell you it is all relative.

There are many books written about my origins and most of them get it wrong. One thing they don't get right enough, however, is the fact that The Dark Arts & Magic School near Hermannstadt, the fabled Scholomance, was indeed everything superstitious Romanians believed it to be and then some.

To be fair to the Romanian villagers and the wandering gypsies, the latter of whom I considered to be my vassals, the fact that a dark magic war was waged between the Scholomance wizard and me for years across the countryside must have been the cause for the plethora of local superstitions in the first place. We fought battles in the dark recesses of the forests, mountains, and caves as we sought each other's annihilation. And, as you might expect, it is the victor's name that lurks behind every superstitious fear: *Gregynia Drakuluj* (Devil's garden), *Gania Drakuluj* (Devil's mountain), *Yadu Drakuluj* (Devil's abyss).

The antagonism between Feurix and myself only arose because of rank jealousy on his part. At the start of my apprenticeship, Feurix embraced and quickly elevated me to the rank of Tenth, the Dragonrider—he who would awaken the beast from the depths of the lake and ride him to cast thunderstorms far and wide. But, given my preternatural talents as nosferatu, he became envious of my easy mastery. Whereas Feurix knew all the secrets of nature, the language of animals, and the alchemy of compounds, he became ever more recalcitrant in imparting their inner workings to me.

I hadn't realized that grudging envy had transformed into vengeful fury when an exercise in necromantic regeneration using the blackest of soul gems turned out to be a deathly booby trap. Feurix had already animated the mummified corpse with a warrior spirit, so that when I sliced open the restraining bands, I found myself under the onslaught of a scimitar wielding demon. I barely escaped thanks to my ingenuity and supernatural reflexes.

Thereafter, it was open warfare. I was determined to stamp out Feurix. Our conflict waged over days and weeks. One day, I'll give the world a step-by-step account of how I defeated the wily, cunning, and masterful Feurix in a book I'd like to entitle *The Full Blood Prince and the Deathly Grotto*. Suffice it to say that it was only when I had won that I realized what I had lost.

I had lost access to the vast knowledge Feurix possessed in the dark and arcane arts. In the shortest of times, he had taught me things that are the stuff of legend today: how to throw neither shadow nor mirror reflection; how to summon elemental power for superhuman strength; how to transform into wolf, dog, bat, and even dust; how to create a mist to shroud my seaward journeys; how to dematerialize to slip through a hairbreadth of space; how to see in the blackest of nights.

But, had I been longer favored with his tutelage, I would have learnt to overcome my glaring limitations. Even today, my power ceases at the coming of the day. Even today, I cannot enter without someone bidding me in. Even today, I must replenish by resting in the soil of my ancestral home; even today, I cannot swim in any form of natural water—be it ocean, river, or lake; Even today, I am helpless as a newborn as I lie in my coffin.

As the years pass, I've come to understand that something is always lost for something gained. Feurix could have taught me so much more had he lived; and yet, his death had become inevitable given his limitations and jealousy. His was a mediocre mind that violently opposed me; mine was the soaring spirit that got prematurely clipped.

(684 words)

6. Describe a topic, idea, or concept you find so engaging that it makes you lose all track of time. Why does it captivate you? What or who do you turn to when you want to learn more?

Mastery.

I have so lived my eternal life, so conceived of all my actions, so as to be Master. In subservience is failure. In mastery is overcoming. In my heart of hearts, I have desired nothing more than becoming the Master of all humanity in order to snatch them out of their lives of self-inflicted violence and suffering and transmute them into a likeness of my being.

Becoming *the* Master is an infinitely consuming task. Thankfully, I Count Dracula have infinite time on hand. But when time stretches out like an endless scroll, it becomes easy, much too easy, to lose track of it. In my life as a Boyar, I became master to the peasants and also the Szigane; yet I would be remiss if I didn't share the fact that I spent a couple of centuries achieving what could have taken mere decades simply because time is never of the essence for me.

Or take my misfortunate foray into England more than a century ago. Prior to orchestrating the arrival of Jonathan Harker to my castle in Transylvania, I had lost myself for decades in the study of everything British. I had mastered the language, the customs, and the idioms. Each and every book on the subject of England that I could lay my hands on, had I devoured. Each and every guest hailing from the British Isles, had I devoured. Yet the second I greeted Jonathan, it became painfully obvious to me that I lacked even the intonation of an Englishman. I realized, yet again, that I knew the grammar and the words, but I knew not the language they spoke. So I redoubled my efforts to absorb everything Jonathan had to offer.

And even though England didn't work out the way I had hoped, not once did anyone there suspect I was anything other than a proper Englishman going about his business in the crowded streets of mighty London, in the midst of the whirl and rush of humanity.

Through the centuries, I have always gravitated to the centers of civilization not simply to feed or prey but with a view to mastering the essential knowledge that makes each civilization dominant in its time. To be a master of all and servant to none requires a painstaking commitment to continuous learning. In ancient Greece, you'd find me in the shadows of the marketplace in the Acropolis lending a keen year to the Sophistic argumentation between Protagoras and Diogenes. In Mauryan India, I partook with King Ashoka in both the massacre at Kalinga as well as in his ensuing adoption of Buddhist tenets. How often, in the Roman Colosseum, did I smuggle in myself as a gladiator to perfect my combat skills as both the large-shielded but single greaved scutarius and also the small-shielded but double-greaved parmularius. When the Yongle Emperor decreed that the Great Wall be built in China, I immersed myself with the engineers to perfect the masonry and construction that enabled the creation of that seventh wonder of the world.

Which brings me to the United States, the current if fleeting wonder of the modern world. It is the epicenter of exponentially proliferating knowledge, the Mecca of invention and innovation. So diverse are the options and avenues for the pursuit of mastery that my immersion in all things American will easily be my longest in any culture, past and present. I am almost in a delirium of anticipation as I consider what majors to explore in college first: shall I learn the psychotropic details of tetrahydrocannabinol in the Cannabis Chemistry major, or develop virtual cognition in the Video Gaming major, or inspect evidence from organismal and ecological perspectives in the Forensics major? Or, better yet, shall I profit from American expediency and triple-major all at once?

I will be like a kid in a candy shop on the college campus, reaching out as often as I can for a taste and a nibble to satisfy my insatiable appetite before I sink my teeth in deep to truly master the subject at hand. Only in mastery is leadership born and does conviction arise.

(689 words. Surely they keep reading beyond 650...!)

7. **Share an essay on any topic of your choice. It can be one you have already written, one that responds to a different prompt, or one of your own design.**

Isn't life and even living life just another form of being Un-dead? Would you rather remain human and march inexorably towards death or would you rather ascend to vampire and live a life more eternal?

It has never failed to surprise me how even the most rational of minds succumb to ignorance when it comes to the gift that I am able to bestow on humanity. People dream fondly of the elixir of eternal life, for a draught of immortality…And yet, when I present it to them, it is sheer hatred, panic, and revulsion that ensues.

The vampire's kiss is a liberation not a curse; it is an elevation not a fall.

It has been rightly said of me that the blood of many races flows in my veins, yet it has been incorrectly assumed that the wars of violence—in which I fought as the lion fights for lordship over all—were my doing or provided cause for my exultation. Nothing can be further from the truth: I hate violence; I hate war. My actions through the millennia have been purely defensive, to protect what is mine.

You could say my existence has often been swept up in whirlpools of blood, and you could also correctly say I have escaped from these not simply unscathed but invigorated and rejuvenated. Yet, I'd like to plead my innocence for any blood spilled in these incessant European wars. I'd like to claim self-defense for any manslaughter associated with my name.

It is no accident that after a careful survey, I chose to settle in the Carpathians and make my abode in an impregnable castle set on the highest mountain and the sheerest cliff. I expected that the sight of the dark, stone edifice perched a thousand feet up on the summit of a yawning precipice would discourage anyone from thoughts of conquest.

And yet, I had discounted the irrepressible violence that bubbles like lava beneath all other elements of human nature. Far from being discouraged by my location and reputation, hordes continually assailed my kingdom. Emboldened by Thor and Wodin, the Ugrics of Iceland assaulted my domain with fell intent, not knowing that whilst they only donned the wolf headdress, I was the true werewolf and summoner of wolves. Then followed the Huns led by Attila, the fiercest of marauders who claimed that in their veins ran the blood of Scythian witches wed to the devil. After I quelled them, I can assure you the only blood that ran was Attila's in my veins. Arpad and his Hungarian Legions came knocking next, swollen with the zeal of the Honfoglalas and dreams of eastward conquest, but him too I absorbed as he lay dreaming on his back in the dark of his tent under a moonless sky. In the Kosovan war, I lurked in the shadows ensuring Sultan Murad of the Ottomans defeated the Crusader army of Hunyadi if only to salvage breathing room and a modicum of rest until the next onslaught on my lands.

And come the onslaughts did. The Magyars, the Lombards, the Avar, the Bulgar, the Turk—they poured by the thousands on my frontiers and I did what I had to do to protect my lands and my vassals. But the irony of it all is that my valorous acts of self-defense have been used to paint me as a bloodthirsty, ravaging, and violent entity whereas nothing could be further from the truth.

How easily humanity forgets that, left to my own devices, my conversion is selective and sensual, seductive and mutual. Far be it from me to visit violence upon my brides or my bondsmen. My embrace has a deliberate voluptuousness that my victim finds thrilling to the core. It is she who arches her back of her own volition. It is she who stretches her slender neck towards my sharp teeth shining white against blood red lips. It is she who swoons feeling my hot breath descend upon her neck. We are of equal desire when I feel her skin begin to tingle under the soft shivering touch of my lips, of equal tension as we await the release promised by the puncture of canines breaking the softest flesh. We become one in the languorous ecstasy that throbs with our eager pumping hearts.

I, Count Dracula, am a lover not a fighter. And the ascension I offer is born of consummation not conflict.

(735 words. So much to say, such little space!)

CHAPTER 4
Rejectionville

VARDHAR UNIVERSITY
Allston • Massachusetts • 02134

Bradley Pittman, Director
Admissions and Financial Aid
Vardhar College, Bridgecam, MA

Dear Count Dracula,

The Committee on Admissions has finished its deliberations for the Regular Admissions applicant pool, and I am very sorry to inform you that we are unable to offer you admission to the incoming freshman class. This decision is no reflection of your achievements and accomplishments, and it is the committee's firm belief that you will find success wherever you choose to go in the fall.

On a personal note, please be advised that while we found your persona of Count Dracula amusing, it does not help you in making a compelling case for your candidature. Yes, we are obliged to evaluate all applications with the same fair and impartial standards that do merit to our institution. And yes, we are obliged to take all claims made by the applicant at face value. However, your file clearly exceeds the bounds of credulity. In your personal statements (we only require one, not seven), you come off as a self-centered egotist whose idea of what colleges are looking for in a candidate is erroneous at best and delusional at worst.

This year, we received a record number of applications, in excess of 39,000! We wish we could admit all the qualified candidates we encountered in the review process, and we understand the hopes and expectations placed on us by students and their families. We are also confident, however, that it is what you bring over the next four years to the college campus of your choice that will pave your future success.

Sincerely,
Bradley Pittman
Dean of Admissions and Financial Aid

Brad Pittman

FORDSTAN UNIVERSITY

San Jose • California • 94088

Angelique Jollinovic,
Director of Admissions
Fordstan University, Fordstan, California

Dear Count Dracula,

I am very sorry to inform you that after a careful review of your application materials, the Admissions Committee is unable to offer you admission to Fordstan University. This decision in no way diminishes the thoughtfulness and care with which you completed your application.

Honestly, we were perplexed by the hopes and dreams your application represents as seen through all the college essays you submitted. We were shocked by the declaration of your vampire abilities and the manner in which you uphold them as a platform for change. We were also confused by what possible academic direction you might pursue given your predisposition for the necrophilic. Finally, your extracurricular activities, if they are to be believed, send a shudder down the spine of any human reader.

If you have any lingering doubts or confusion about the admissions process, please visit the FAQ page on our college website.

Thank you for applying to Fordstan. We enjoyed learning about you and are perturbed at the thought that you will likely thrive wherever your educational pursuits take you.

Sincerely,
Angelique Jollinovitch
Director of Admissions

THE UNIVERSITY OF CAGOCHI

Cagochi · Illinois · 37606

Dean of Admissions and Financial Aid
The University of Cagochi
Cagochi, Illinois

Dear Applicant,

The Admissions Committee has finished its review of all applications. We regret to inform you that we were unable to reserve a spot for you in the incoming freshman class. This year's applicant pool was by far the strongest in University of Cagochi history. This means that we could not extend an offer to many worthy applicants such as yourself.

While his decision may come as a disappointment to you, we hope that you will pursue your dreams and aspirations with the same enthusiasm and initiative you showed in your application with us.

Please accept our best wishes as you pursue your educational goals.

Sincerely,
John Annistone, Ed. D.
Dean of Admissions and Financial Aid

Johnny Annistone

Kedu

Dean of Undergraduate Admissions
Kedu University
Hamdur, North Carolina

Dear Count Dracula,

Thank you for applying for admission to Kedu University. I am so sorry to tell you that we are unable to invite you to be a freshman at Kedu next fall.

Nothing I can say will ease your disappointment, but rest assured that our decision is more a reflection of the large and talented applicant pool this year and less so a judgment about the merits of your application.

We had to disappoint many deserving and accomplished young men and women as also yourself. My staff and I are impressed by your many decades (and centuries!) of balancing a challenging workload with all the various nocturnal commitments you claim to be so proficient at. It would be no exaggeration to state that we were uniformly impressed with the long list of achievements pertaining to your incisive and assimilative qualities. We truly wish we had room for the likes of you on our campus.

I know that this is not the letter you were hoping to receive. But I know that you have unlimited potential for success in your chosen endeavors and am sanguine that you will find your way forward regardless of this setback.

Sincerely,
Thomas Hardy
Dean of Undergraduate Admissions

Tommy "Beans" Hardy

TONPRINCE
UNIVERSITY

Dean of Admission
Tonprince College of Arts and Science
Tonprince, New Jersey

Dear Dracula,

It is with regret that I have to inform you that we are not able to admit you to Tonprince University for the upcoming year. The admissions process is a difficult and trying one for students and families, and you are likely disappointed with our decision. We received well over 37,000 applications this year and it is no exaggeration to state that we could have filled many Tonprinces with the thousands of outstanding candidates who applied.

I appreciate that you might find it challenging to accept that you are not among the chosen few. We have been diligent, thoughtful, and careful over the past three months while reviewing each and every application. As we do every year, we spared no effort to weigh each student's achievements individually as well as in a comparative manner that takes into consideration the differences among the 10685 schools and 163 countries represented in the pool.

While you present us with a truly unique set of credentials, it is the committee's belief that your path to knowledge and advancement lies elsewhere. As evidenced by your personal essays, you have a unique set of achievements, talents, and skills. However, we remain unconvinced that any of the qualities that you boast of in your arsenal are college worthy. Reading your application made it clear to us that the horizon of your success exceeds the bounds of a college experience.

The committee's conclusion is not a referendum on your worth, and it does not reflect on your potential of future success. I imagine you are hearing heartening news from other institutions and have many delectable choices at hand.

Please note that this decision is final and this letter our final correspondence. It would serve everyone's interests if you keep from giving us a visitation.

Thank you for your interest in Tonprince.

Sincerely,
Henry Fondanovich
Dean of Admission

CHAPTER 5
Dracula Searches for College Essay Help

Shock.

It was a novel sensation. I hadn't felt this way since Feurix double-crossed me by making me incantate the wrong spell by the Dragon Lake in Transylvania all those centuries ago.

Shock.

Picture me with a glazed, wide eyed, and uncomprehending look—not unlike the one I provoke in my victims when they realize too late that I am not just myth but also menace materialized in the undead flesh.

Rejected. *Me?!* Count freakin' Dracula?!!

How dare they reject me, Prince of Darkness, Immortal Overlord, Monarch of the midnight hellions?

Not one acceptance. Not one "Congratulations." Not one "We are delighted to admit you to the class of…"!

Truly, I was unable to process the onslaught of negation. The more I walked back through my application, the foggier became my mind. Where had I gone wrong? What could I have done differently?

After getting over my initial reaction of shock, I felt anger bubble up like the lava in Mt. Krakatoa waiting to erupt and consume all those who dared reject my application. I was going to take down names and chart out a nationwide revenge tour, nightly visitations to suck the blood out of all the self-important admissions committee reprobates.

But day was breaking out and I had to go lay in my coffin. And after I had slept on it, I emerged the next night with a different perspective. Perhaps my application overlooked some vital aspect; perhaps in my overconfidence, I failed to deliver some non-negotiable element.

I revisited the rejection letters. I read them over and over again.

It became clear that more than anything, all admissions committees had found my college essays objectionable. What I had considered to be seven gems sparkling with the spectrum of my unique brilliance, committees had read as seven duds that damned my candidacy.

Other than the fact some letters expressed disbelief about my really being Count Dracula, most rejections sang the same refrain: incomprehension about why I want to be in college and what I might possibly want to learn in college.

And they all referenced my college essays.

The College Essay did me in!

Now, one thing you need to know about me is that if I fail at first (which I hardly ever do), then you can rest assured that I will sink my teeth into the subject until I succeed. That is my Dracula way.

I had already decided to apply to college again. And this time, I would do everything it takes to gain admission.

However, I was faced with a problem: I had written the best possible college essays I could have. They were personal, they were true, and they sure as hell showed me off as a unique specimen of being. The way I procreate my species, the manner in which I grew from my Van Helsing setback, how Lucy opened my eyes to the excitement of the unknown—these and other topics had I explored with verve and panache in my writing.

And yet, these same essays had worked against me and ensured that I got nothing but rejections.

And here, dear reader, I had yet another novel sensation: I realized I needed help. I didn't know how to fix my essays by myself.

Yay, internet!

I googled "how to write The College Essay," and sifted my way through the thousands of guidelines, formats, suggestions, and samples.

The more I read, the more confusing everything became regarding the form, structure, and content of The College Essay.

But the more I read, the clearer it became that I would be best served by hiring an expert in College Essay writing to walk me through the process.

The internet was proliferating with this new breed of professional, one who promised to know not only the ins and outs of the application process but also the nuts and bolts of how to write a winning college essay.

And of all the potential work-for-hire listings I came across, the one that stuck with me was the one I found on essayt.com: Dr. Van Sood.

I know, I know…I'm a creature of habit and a slave to the familiar. What are the chances he's related?

CHAPTER 6
Please Understand the Purpose, Dracula!

College Essay Writing Services
123 Pleasant Road, Pleasantville, USA
(212) 555 1234
https://www.essayt.com
(Date undisclosed)

John Carmody
Attorney at Large
Sears Tower, Penthouse Suite
Chicago, IL 60666

Dear John Carmody,

I hope this letter finds you well.

Consider this communique an FYI in case something unforeseen or unusual happens to me in the near future. I do not mean to sound dramatic but there has been a curious development, one which I am still trying to wrap my head around. You might feel skepticism and most likely incredulity as you read what I am about to relate below—but, please know that I am sane of mind and sound of body.

As you know, I offer my services to help college applicants with writing The College Essay. While the bulk of my clients find their way to me through word of mouth referrals, a significant number discover my services through the portal essayt.com. As you can imagine, I have had all manner of people from around the world query me through the website, and I have been fortunate to work with some of the most enthusiastic, promising and talented candidates.

My latest client does not lack enthusiasm nor talent, but I would not call him promising for I don't quite know what his promise might be. I just want to be sure that if he is who he says he is, then I have kept a detailed record of our interactions in case I am struck down by untimely misfortune.

My client professes to be Count Dracula.

There is no joke here.

The gentleman in question presents himself as you might imagine Count Dracula to be. He is tall and pale, dressed in old fashioned black on black formal clothing. You would think he just stepped out of a funeral service except that the cut and threads of his bespoke attire speaks of money, lots of it. He has dark, piercing eyes that switch between being clear one instant and bloodshot the next. But that is not what is most unsettling. What really freaks me out is that I am not sure how old he is. At our first meeting, I could have sworn he was a concerned grandpa, what with his bushy white hair and eyebrows. Yet, the next time we met, he presented as robust, dark haired and this side of forty. It was the same man, revitalized and rejuvenated.

I have read his college essays, the ones he sent with all the applications that got him universally rejected. One thing is clear, whoever he might be, he is applying to college as Count Dracula. There is no tongue in cheek here.

The essays are all over the place. Count Dracula or not, he will benefit from my help. And so, I've decided to guide him in his college essay writing process. I hope he is receptive to constructive criticism. Below is a record of our first meeting, transcribed from the audio recording I have stored in my bank locker in case you ever need it for evidence.

Sincerely,

Dr. Van Sood, Ph.D.
https://essayt.com

CAN YOU PLEASE UNDERSTAND THE PURPOSE OF THE
COLLEGE ESSAY, DRACULA?

————————————————————————————————

A Recording of Dr. Van Sood's Informational Session
with Count Dracula

By

Dr. Van Sood

Cast of Characters

Count Dracula	A Vampire, ageless, from Transylvania
Dr. Van Sood	A man in his late 40s;
	College Essay Writing Expert

Scene

Dr. Van Sood's Home Office, somewhere in Long Island.

Time

The present.

ACT I

Scene 1

SETTING: We are in the home office of Doctor Van Sood in a nice looking suburban neighborhood not far from New York City. There is an elegant L-shaped computer desk backstage left. The corner of the desk is away from the audience, and the chair behind the desk faces the entrance to the office upstage right. Downstage center is a sofa arrangement with an understated Victorian flavor: a two-seater sofa and an armchair, a rug and a coffee table with a couple of large books. The space is framed by bookcases to give the feel of erudition. The vibe of the place is academic but also could serve as a psychologist's office.

AT RISE: DR. VAN SOOD is at his computer terminal and scrolling through a bunch of writing. He checks his watch, swivels to check his watch and then the entrance. He gets up to unlock the entrance door and sticks his head out to check the hallway. He locks the door and returns to his work. His foot taps nervously—he is clearly agitated or anxious.

COUNT DRACULA materializes inside the door and approaches the desk in complete silence. Oblivious to his presence, Dr. Van Sood works for a moment oblivious, then swivels to check his watch and the entrance…

DR. VAN SOOD

(startled, springing to his feet, breathing heavily in fear.)

Oh my god! How did you—when did you…Oh Christ, you startled me!

COUNT DRACULA

I have an appointment.

DR. VAN SOOD

Yes, of course…most certainly. But, how did you get in?

COUNT DRACULA

An invitation is all I have ever needed.

(Dr. Van Sood composes himself as best as he can. He offers his hand.)

DR. VAN SOOD

Dr. Van Sood at your service.

(They shake hands. The clasp lingers long enough to make Dr. Van Sood uncomfortable. He pulls his hand out, laughs nervously and directs Dracula to the sofas)

Your hand is…cold! Please, have a seat.

(Dracula sits on the love seat, and Dr. Van Sood takes the arm chair.)

Thank you for coming. Usually, I'd ask you to tell me a bit about your school, what you like, dislike, and the such but you have been out of school for a while. Well, let us begin. I've read all your essays. Did you have time to look over my comments?

COUNT DRACULA

Yes. Your comments are very harsh. Critical.

                    DR. VAN SOOD

          (nervous)

Critical?! Not at all. it is just feedback, what works, what
does not work, don't miss the forest for the trees, things
like that.

                   COUNT DRACULA

So if I make the fixes, is it good to go?

                    DR. VAN SOOD

Well, not exactly. See—there is nothing wrong with the
quality of your writing. You write well. Grammar, style,
structure. In fact, you are quite an advanced writer.

                   COUNT DRACULA

          (menacing)

But?

                    DR. VAN SOOD

          (hesitates then decides to speak the
          truth)

Your essays—great as they are—**your essays miss the
Purpose.**

                   COUNT DRACULA

I answered each prompt exactly as it asked.

                    DR. VAN SOOD

Of course.

                    (he retrieves a manila folder from his
                    desk, and hands it to Dracula. He is
                    comfortable now as he launches into his
                    sales pitch: he's said this many times
                    over and to many clients.)

A hardcopy of your essays with all the feedback. The first
sheet has the common application prompts.

                    (waits for Dracula to extract the sheet
                    with the prompts.)

Seven prompts. Seven different questions. But—are they really that different?

(dramatic pause)

In fact, All the questions are ONE question: **What can you tell about yourself in 650 words or less that will convince me you belong on my amazing campus with my amazing students?**

COUNT DRACULA

I have answered that question over and over again.

DR VAN SOOD

But have you really? Let me rephrase the question being asked: What interests, experiences, and/or pursuits can you bring to enrich the campus experience and the lives of your fellow college students?

COUNT DRACULA

I've addressed this in all my essays.

DR VAN SOOD

Your first essay is about converting everyone into vampires. Your second is about how you failed to convert Mina Harker. In the third essay, you claim you are single-handedly responsible for gender liberation. The fourth is about how you got obsessed with Lucy the somnambulist. The next one, you annihilate Feurix and lose access to arcane knowledge. Essay number six is about your obsession with Mastery through the millenia. And the last essay is basically a rant about spilling blood through the centuries.

(dramatic pause)

Now, which of these do you think would make an admissions officer go, "Wow, I really need this candidate on my campus!"?

COUNT DRACULA

All of them show how I am unique and talented.

DR VAN SOOD

But is it the kind of unique that leads to open-armed embrace or crucifix-armed rejection?

> (Silence as Dracula sifts through the folder and mulls over the fact that he was rejected by each and every college he applied to.)

COUNT DRACULA

So what's the secret?

DR. VAN SOOD

The secret lies in understanding one truth: The College Essay is not an essay at all! The College Essay is a misnomer for what should actually be called "A Short Story about the Journey of Your Life"!

COUNT DRACULA

Story? But I have written so many stories in my college essays—about Mina, Lucy, and Feurix.

DR. VAN SOOD

Ah yes, my dear Count—but stories with what purpose? No matter the prompt, no matter the story, the purpose remains the same.

> (sits on armchair, triumphant)

COUNT DRACULA

And that purpose being?

DR. VAN SOOD

What you have learned on your journey so far, what experiences you have had in your journey so far, **how do these experiences motivate you for the college experience, which includes not just taking what the college offers but giving the college what it desires.**

COUNT DRACULA

What does the college desire?

                         DR. VAN SOOD

The college desires a candidate who is going to be an
asset to the college community, someone who will contribute
their unique interests and perspective to enrich the
college experience of all other students. And you have 650
words to tell a story that will convince them you are that
type of candidate.

                         COUNT DRACULA

                    (agitated)

650 words? Impossible.

                         DR. VAN SOOD

A story that also showcases the experiences you have
pursued in your life. A story that shows how your life so
far has fostered interests for your future.

                         COUNT DRACULA

                    (seething now)

In 650 words?

                         DR VAN SOOD

                    (superior smile)

Or less.

(Dracula springs up and is behind Dr. Van Sood's armchair
in the blink of an eye. His left hand pushes Van Sood's
head sideways to expose the neck.)

                         COUNT DRACULA

                    (snarling, canines exposed, bending Close
                    to Dr. Van Sood's neck)

I will not be mocked.

                         DR. VAN SOOD

Please, please! I only speak the truth!

                         COUNT DRACULA

What you speak of is impossible.

DR. VAN SOOD

Please! Listen to me. I have worksheets. Just follow my process. It had literally worked for thousands of college applicants. I guarantee it will help you craft a winning college essay.

COUNT DRACULA

And if your process fails?

DR. VAN SOOD

A great story that serves the purpose cannot fail.

(Count Dracula relents and releases his grip on Dr. Van Sood.)

COUNT DRACULA

What makes you so certain?

DR. VAN SOOD

I've literally walked thousands through the process and helped them craft a story of their journey so far, a story that stands out because it is authentic and also memorable.

COUNT DRACULA

Very well. Let us get to it. But this had better work…

(Dr. Van Sood gets up and goes to his desk, all the while keeping a wary eye on Count Dracula. He retrieves a folder marked "Essayt.com Workshop and hands it to the Count. Dracula quickly leafs through the contents, then offers a wicked grin)

…Or I'll be coming for you.

(BLACKOUT)

(END OF SCENE)

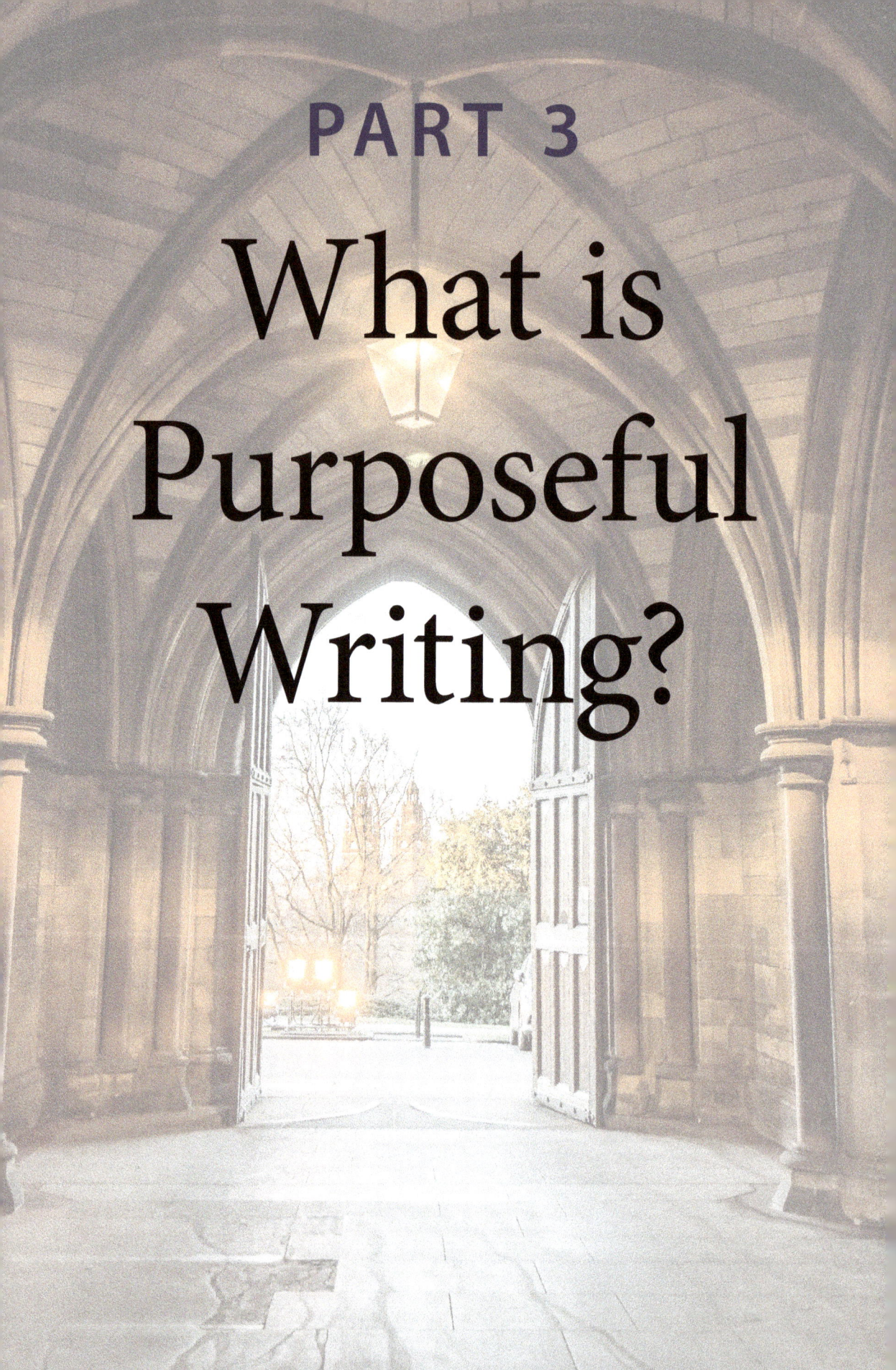

PART 3

What is Purposeful Writing?

CHAPTER 7
Your Turn: Identify the Errors in "Great Writing"

Anyone reading this book should be excited not only to gain insight into what makes a great story but also what makes for great writing.

With that in mind, I invite you, dear reader, to put on your thinking cap and play a little game with me. I have identified various moments in Dracula's writing that are either well composed, need addressing, or weaken the essays: can you figure out why?

Grab a pencil, read the highlighted portions, and write down in the accompanying boxes what you think needs to be addressed and/or fixed.

Then, in the following chapter, please cross-check your answers with the ones I have provided.

Note: This exercise will serve you well outside of the scope of just The College Essay. Be thoughtful in your answers, and you will gain insight into the art and craft of effective writing.

1. **Some students have a background, identity, interest, or talent that is so meaningful that their application would be incomplete without it. If this sounds like you, then please share your story.**

(Were they thinking of me, Count Dracula, when they created this prompt? I am unique in each of these categories: my background, my identity, my interest, my talent! Quite obviously my application would be incomplete without it.)

Here goes:

Unlike mere mortals[1], my consciousness doesn't begin at birth. I have always been Count Dracula. I am not of mother born nor of father seeded. My existence knows neither childhood nor aging. I am extra-racial but not extra-terrestrial (at least not to my knowledge). Popular culture considers me to be Carpathian or Romanian, Szekelian or Hungarian, Dacian or Thracian—but, I ask you, can you truly pigeonhole the ethnicity of a shape-shifting, form-changing, mutant-morphing creature of the night such as myself? I don't think so.[2]

1. The good: _____

_____

_____

1. The bad: _____

_____

_____

_____

2. The good: _____

_____

_____

Which brings me to my unique identity. I am the original vampire.[3] While my condition has been seen as an affliction or disease or some grievous wrong against the natural order of being, I can assure you I live and breathe with the same purpose my acolyte Darwin recognized more than a century ago: survival and procreation. Though in my superhuman adaptability, the propagation of my species aka[4] vampires is advanced biology.

3. The good: _____

_____

_____

3. The bad: _____

_____

_____

_____

4. The bad: _____

_____

_____

Yes, I am a lover and make love but the sex is just for sex's sake.[5] It is the bite—the transfusion and transmission—that creates my progeny.

5. The bad: _____

_____

_____

I never give birth, but I rebirth humans into my likeness of being.

The selection of which human to elevate into my higher plane of existence relies on my innate talent[6] of being able to penetrate all defenses that suppress true desire. Not everyone desires the exhilaration of vampiric existence. Not everyone is worthy of such elevation.

6. Address: _____

_____

_____

But those that desire me and desire what I offer wonder, "How will I ever know if I am worthy of Count Dracula's bite? And how in Satan's name will Dracula be able to find me?"

Well, fear not, needy little homo sapien.[7] My true talent, nay gift, is magnetic attraction to your innermost, deepest and darkest desires.[8] Desires you know you have, desires you are ashamed to have, and desires you didn't know you have.

7. The bad: _____

_____

_____

_____

8. The bad: _____

_____

_____

But I, Count Dracula, know your darkest desires! I feel them! I am drawn to them! It is your desire I feast on as I suck your blood! And if the rapture of our commingling is worthy enough, you are in! you are transfigured into my likeness and join my legion.[9]

9. The bad: _____

_____

_____

In all honesty, I consider this talent to be my greatest gift.

(375 words…too short. I don't know what else to write.)

2. **The lessons we take from obstacles we encounter can be fundamental to later success. Recount a time when you faced a challenge, setback, or failure. How did it affect you, and what did you learn from the experience?**

From the countless campaigns I waged over the centuries—as King and Commander in the Dark Ages, as Count and C.E.O in the Modern Ages—the setback that makes me most rueful is a fleeting episode in the saga of my somnambulist conquests. In England, in 1899, I identified nothing less than a woman worthy of ascension to Queen of the Undead.[10] Her name was Mina Harker. Her pent up desires overwhelmed me with their unabashed embrace of the forbidden.[11]

10. The bad: (Diction) _____

_____

_____

11. The bad: _____

_____

_____

My very first glimpse of Mina, and I realized why London had been calling me all along, why I had endured passage in choppy seas, why I had acquired properties all across that grimy city, why[12] I had been putting myself out of my comfort zone by sleeping in rudimentary boxes filled with my native soil. Here she was, my wondrous Wilhelmina, kin of my kin, yearning for the liberation that only my teeth sunk deep into her neck[13] could deliver.

12. The bad: (Grammar) _____

_____

_____

13. The good: _____

_____

_____

13. The bad: _____

_____

_____

But to get to Mina, to indoctrinate and to assimilate Mina,[14] to absorb Mina and to transform her into becoming the queen of my coterie of undead countesses proved to be an abject failure.

14. The bad: _____

_____

_____

My objectives were constantly thwarted by a bunch of do-gooders led by the nefarious Dr. Van Helsing, the luckiest devil to ever have crossed my path and survived.[15] At me he thrust garlic, at me he brandished The Cross, at me he tossed sacramental wafers. And guess what?[16] Because he found me repulsed, he thought his religion had power over me!

15. Address: _____

_____

_____

16. The bad: _____

_____

_____

If only Helsing knew that I was affected not by any mystical force of his moronic[17] charms but because of allergens! Brandish me your crucifix today, Van Helsing, and I'll brandish you my Epipen.

17. The bad: _____

_____

_____

But I digress. Truth be told, even today I tip my hat to the resolve of the Stoker gang for making that concerted effort that thwarted my conquest of Mina.

They burst upon me during that primal moment when I had Mina entranced, ensconced in my bosom, and suckling the very life blood from the freshly incised artery in my chest. I was in a rapture, a delight swelling up in me that would surely explode to fill up the universe itself.[18]

18. The good: _____

_____

_____

18. The bad: _____

_____

_____

Mina had succumbed, her barriers had dissipated, and she was eager to merge. Perhaps I let my guard down and lingered too long in the bliss of this Vampire baptism. Perhaps I fell prey to my own overconfidence, but I failed to hear them until it was too late.

To my dismay, they were armed with all of the aforementioned allergens that debilitate me. I got so furious at the interruption of my bodacious banquet that I couldn't think straight and barely curbed my involuntary reaction of pouncing on the gang to tear them to shreds.

But sanity prevailed and I made my exit. At the time, I was rather sanguine about finding Mina and having her all to myself in the near future.

How wrong was I!

They worked in concert to infiltrate and booby trap all my coffin-boxes around London—in Carfax, Bermondsey, Mile End, Walworth. The men even had the temerity to lay an ambush for me at my abode in Piccadilly, armed as always with those god-forsaken allergens hidden in their crucifixes and wafers. Long story short, I was chased out of London and stalked all the way to my home in Transylvania. And Mina, I was never able to deliver the poor soul from her mortal existence, never able to give her what she truly desired—becoming Queen of the Undead and ruling by my side.

This failure affected me deeply. Despite my superior being, I was thwarted by mere mortals. I took the defeat to heart (no pun intended) and conducted a clinical analysis of why I had failed in my conquest of Mina and, more importantly, how I would never fail again in my future endeavors.

After much reflection, I realized that my enterprise suffered from inadequate preparation, planning, and execution in four domains: delegation, anticipation, underestimation, and, last but not least, medication.[19]

19. The good: (Structure) _____

_____

_____

Delegation. I had gone solo. Never again. Granted, I am invincible; yet, I cannot be at multiple places at once. When faced by an enemy united in their numbers and coordinated in their actions, I cannot outmaneuver them by myself. For my expedition to London, I should have conscripted the services of the Three Sisters instead of leaving them behind to toy with Jonathan Harker. I should have used that profligate lunatic Renfield to greater advantage instead of too soon snapping his neck. I should have created my own little army of progeny to command and marshall in the field, disposing of them[20] once they'd performed their duties.

Anticipation: Sure, I was strategic in my plans, from the purchase of properties in prime locations, to shipping more than adequate supplies of native-soil coffins, to preying on my chosen women at the most opportune times. However, I paid scant regard to the possibility that my foes, though weaklings in most regards, were equally endowed with strategic acumen. While they anticipated my every move, I failed to examine their countermoves—they were playing chess not checkers. It was a humbling realization. From that moment forward, I always put myself in my adversaries' shoes before deciding on my next course of action.

Underestimation: I believed my adversary, the Stoker gang, to be weak just because they seemed to rely too much on religious icons. I was too quick to peg them with the religious fanatics I'd been encountering for centuries, people wed to superstition and dying for divine intervention. But Drs. Van Helsing, Seward et al. turned out to be confounding creatures whose swiftness for scientific experimentation was instrumental in defeating me. They figured out that the soil in my coffin had nutrients essential to my regeneration. They almost saved Lucy by administering blood transfusions. They collated multiple records of their interactions with me in order to analyze my predatory habits and create plans based on cold, hard logic. They exploited my telepathic bond with Mina. Underestimating their scientific acumen cost me victory. After London, I resolved: Never again.

Medication: if only they'd invented the epipen in 1899 instead of 1987. I go nowhere without it now. Come at me, crucifix! Whatchoo got, garlic?! Watch out, wafers![21] I have privately funded the development of multidose autoinjectors (yes, yes, patent violations and all that)[22] and I never leave home without it. You could say that the epipen is the only gun I'll ever need to carry into a battle and Epinephrine is my silver bullet.

22. The bad: (Details) _____

_____

_____

(1102 words! Too long. I don't know what to cut…)

3. Reflect on a time when you questioned or challenged a belief or idea. What prompted your thinking? What was the outcome?

From the very onset of my existence,[23] I have challenged the notion of binary sex and sexuality. Mine is a creative biology that literally transforms the site of desire from the conventional erogenous zones (genitalia, for most of you mortals) to those twin orifices on the neck: delicious, blood-tinged, and pulsing for more.

23. The bad: (False Claim) _____

_____

_____

The world regards my conquests as victims, but they could not be more wrong! Properly speaking, both my "victim" and I are submissive partners, submitting[24] to each other in turns. The blood I drink from your neck, the blood you drink from my bosom[25]—a cycle of orgiastic becoming.

24. The bad: _____

_____

_____

25. The bad: _____

_____

_____

In my lovemaking, I am always subverting the heterodoxy of sexuality, turning on its head the belief system that males are males and females are females. I am the sole progenitor, I am both mother and father, father and mother, both husband and wife, and wife and husband. All my hordes[26] are procreated from me and me alone.

26. The bad: _____

_____

_____

People believe that bloodlust is what makes us vampire. They couldn't be further from the truth. What makes us vampires is the act of disrobing the garments imposed by society. Humans tend to wear the clothes chosen for them from the time of birth to the time of death: male to be blue to be boy, female to be pink to be girl.[27]

27. The good: (Style) _____

_____

_____

To be vampire is to be black to be more.[28]

28. The good: _____

_____

_____

To be vampire is to be a being without binary.

I wouldn't stir up a fuss about this except for the fuss stirred up by your kind, the males amongst the mortals. So much effort is expended in all parts of the world to hide the fact that the limitations of the roles males can play—and the roles females cannot play—is based on nothing more than arbitrary destiny.[29]

29. Address: (Clarity) _____

_____

_____

One might say that I have chafed at this global conspiracy to keep men up and women down—for centuries I have played the role of liberator, turning women to my cause.

I submit, with a sense of understated humility, that I, Count Dracula, am the first feminist.

So the question becomes: what has been the outcome of my concerted efforts at undermining and exposing male complicity in the global oppression of others?

Clearly, I have been demonized by the male world. Theirs has been an unflagging smear-campaign fueled by the deep seated resentment of (male) power brokers around the planet. Their world might be divided in its representations of the devil as a tempting and sinful agent, but it is united in its portrayal of Dracula as a malevolent and unnatural beast.

Yet, there has been another outcome, a transformative change in society for which I am responsible but for which I will forever remain its unsung hero. I speak of the inexorable shift away from the oppression of patriarchy through the centuries.

Were it not for my late night jaunts across the world and into the bedchambers of the powerful, the world would not be in the state of gender liberation that it is today. The amount of research, planning, and execution I have undertaken in terms of identifying the best placed victims for vampiric conversion merits a Nobel Prize in Physiology or Medicine, perhaps even in Economics.[30]

30. The bad: (Tone) _____

_____

_____

I have taken the best of the best females to the next level of biology and reduced the most vainglorious of men to compliance.[31]

31. The bad: _____

_____

_____

So many wars have I averted by a pointed nibble, simple possession and quick conversion of the right person at the right place and the right time.

This makes me wonder: why not the Nobel Peace Prize for Count Dracula?

(592 words. Getting there!)

4. Reflect on something that someone has done for you that has made you happy or thankful in a surprising way. How has this gratitude affected or motivated you?

Lucy Westenra.[32]

32. The good: _____
_____
_____

If I might be allowed to claim that Mina Harker was my first experience of love at first sight, then I would like to aver that meeting Lucy in her unguarded somnambulance surprised me with a happiness I hadn't thought possible.

I will never cease to be grateful for what snowy Lucy in her white nightdress gave me that night in the ruins of St. Mary's Church. Little did I know as I lurked behind her bench watching the rays of the full moon slide down her exposed skin, that it was I who was about to be ravished..

What Lucy gave to me was the realization that there is always something new and unknown waiting to be discovered no matter how jaded by immortality you[33] might be. Excuse me—how jaded by immortality I might be.

33. The bad: _____
_____
_____

After all, when you have lived as long as I have, you have pretty much done it all, experienced it all. Believe it or not, being eternal has its drawbacks—not least of which is the fact that one is hard-pressed to find any truly new, undiscovered, and unexpected pleasure in this monotony called walking dead.[34]

34. The bad: (Purpose) _____
_____
_____

For how long had I been yearning to be yanked from the repetition of the same, and how unexpected was finding a novel intoxication in Lucy's embrace.

Simply put: I had never clasped any of my tender targets, never first sunk my eager canines into the soft curve of exposed neck whilst they were in that mysterious state of simultaneous consciousness and unconsciousness: the sleepwalker's drift.

You see, I had no idea that Lucy was in sleep-walking condition[35] when she arched her back, stretched out her arms to clasp me by the neck, and drew me down from behind the bench for my first taste of her.[36]

35. The bad: _____

_____

_____

36. The bad: _____

_____

_____

And how unexpectedly explosive the experience was! All the frustrations of my seaborne journey on that cursed ship Demeter, all the tension of my novel venture in that undiscovered country called England, all my perpetual watchful wariness of being a stranger in a strange land—all of it dissolved into an ecstasy of unbidden fireworks to rival the merriment of the dancing stars in the night sky above us. I became a mindless, powerless entity as her blood pulsed in my mouth, losing all reserve and all caution, wanting this moment to last forever, wanting to howl at the moon for eternity.[37]

37. The good: _____

_____

_____

And how full of delight was the process of somnambulist conversion! Heretofore, I had been using the mesmeric power of my glowing eyes to entrance my victims, to make them swoon with unbidden desire for my suck. But Lucy's blood,[38] as it pulsed its way down my throat, had me entranced with a whole host of sensations I hadn't known existed. The ecstasy was beyond belief. I lost all sense of time and space. I was floating in pure delight.

38. The bad: _____

_____

_____

Only to be interrupted by Mina Harker!

Despite my raging fury at the untimely disruption, I held back from attacking Mina. Because, you see, I was working out how to relive my titillating tryst with Lucy. Ah, dear admissions committee, I wanted Lucy again and again and again. She had become my dependency.[39]

39. The bad: _____

_____

_____

The only question I kept asking myself was: how to prolong my carnal cavort[40] with sleepwalking Lucy without completely converting her into a vampire?

40. The bad: _____

_____

_____

Well, fortune was on my side. It was my very enemies led by Van Helsing who unwittingly ensured that Lucy would be replenished after our trysts to sleepwalk yet another night! In their zeal to revive her, they daily administered blood transfusions not knowing that they were merely replenishing her for our nighttime affairs.

And yet, all things human come to end. When Lucy crossed over and even before she was executed in cold blood by the Helsing group, I made a solemn promise: to do everything in my power to research the science behind somnambulist conversion.[41]

41. Address: _____

_____

_____

For this unexpected and novel ecstasy, I will forever be grateful to you, my sweet sleepwalking Lucy.

(670 words. Practice makes perfect!)

5. Discuss an accomplishment, event, or realization that sparked a period of personal growth and a new understanding of yourself or others.

Albert, one of my favorite conversions, is often quoted for saying something that I personally told him when regaling him with tales from my days at the Scholomance in Romania. "Great spirits have always encountered violent opposition from mediocre minds." I came up with that quote first—you can ask him yourself if you find him, but he'll probably tell you it is all relative.[42]

---

42. The good: _____

_____

_____

There are many books written about my origins and most of them get it wrong. One thing they don't get right enough, however, is the fact that The Dark Arts & Magic School near Hermannstadt, the fabled Scholomance, was indeed everything superstitious Romanians believed it to be and then some.

To be fair to the Romanian villagers and the wandering gypsies, the latter of whom I considered to be my vassals, the fact that a dark magic war was waged between the Scholomance wizard and me for years across the countryside must have been the cause for the plethora of local superstitions in the first place. We fought battles in the dark recesses of the forests, mountains, and caves as we sought each other's annihilation. And, as you might expect, it is the victor's name that lurks behind every superstitious fear: *Gregynia Drakuluj* (Devil's garden), *Gania Drakuluj* (Devil's mountain), *Yadu Drakuluj* (Devil's abyss).

The antagonism between Feurix and myself only arose because of rank jealousy on his part. At the start of my apprenticeship, Feurix embraced and quickly elevated me to the rank of Tenth, the Dragonrider—he who would awaken the beast from the depths of the lake and ride him to cast thunderstorms far and wide. But, given my preternatural talents as nosferatu, he became envious of my easy mastery. Whereas Feurix knew all the secrets of nature, the language of animals, and the alchemy of compounds, he became ever more recalcitrant in imparting their inner workings to me.

I hadn't realized that grudging envy had transformed into vengeful fury when an exercise in necromantic regeneration using the blackest of soul gems turned out to be a deathly booby trap. Feurix had already animated the mummified corpse with a warrior spirit, so that when I sliced open the restraining bands, I found myself under the onslaught of a scimitar wielding demon. I barely escaped thanks to my ingenuity and supernatural reflexes.

Thereafter, it was open warfare. I was determined to stamp out Feurix.[43] Our conflict waged over days and weeks. One day, I'll give the world a step-by-step account of how I defeated the wily, cunning, and masterful Feurix in a book I'd like to entitle *The Full Blood Prince and the Deathly Grotto.*[44] Suffice it to say that it was only when I had won that I realized what I had lost.

43. The bad: _____

_____

_____

44. Address: (Structure) _____

_____

_____

I had lost access to the vast knowledge Feurix possessed in the dark and arcane arts. In the shortest of times, he had taught me things that are the stuff of legend today: how to[45] throw neither shadow nor mirror reflection; how to summon elemental power for superhuman strength; how to transform into wolf, dog, bat, and even dust; how to create a mist to shroud my seaward journeys; how to dematerialize to slip through a hairbreadth of space; how to see in the blackest of nights.

45. The good: (Style) _____

_____

_____

But, had I been longer favored with his tutelage, I would have learnt to overcome my glaring limitations. Even today, my power ceases at the coming of the day. Even today,[46] I cannot enter without someone bidding me in. Even today, I must replenish by resting in the soil of my ancestral home; even today, I cannot swim in any form of natural water—be it ocean, river, or lake; Even today, I am helpless as a newborn as I lie in my coffin.

46. The good: (Style) _____

_____

_____

As the years pass, I've come to understand that something is always lost for something gained. Feurix could have taught me so much more had he lived; and yet, his death had become inevitable given his limitations and jealousy. His was a mediocre mind that violently opposed me; mine was the soaring spirit that got prematurely clipped.[47]

47. The good: (Style) _____

_____

_____

(681 words)

6. Describe a topic, idea, or concept you find so engaging that it makes you lose all track of time. Why does it captivate you? What or who do you turn to when you want to learn more?

Mastery.

I have so lived my eternal life, so conceived of all my actions, so as to be Master. In subservience is failure. In mastery is overcoming. In my heart of hearts, I have desired nothing more than becoming the Master of all humanity in order to snatch them out of their lives of self-inflicted violence and suffering and transmute them into a likeness of my being.[48]

48. Address: _____

_____

_____

Becoming the Master is an infinitely consuming task. Thankfully, I Count Dracula have infinite time on hand. But when time stretches out like an endless scroll, it becomes easy, much too easy, to lose track of it.[49] In my life as a Boyar, I became master to the Peasants and also the Szigane; yet I would be remiss if I didn't share the fact that I spent a couple of centuries achieving what could have taken mere decades simply because time is never of the essence for me.

49. The bad: (Language) _____

_____

_____

Or take my misfortunate foray into England more than a century ago. Prior to orchestrating the arrival of Jonathan Harker to my castle in Transylvania, I had lost myself for decades in the study of everything British. I had mastered the language, the customs, and the idioms. Each and every book on the subject of England that I could lay my hands on, had I devoured.[50] Each and every guest hailing from the British Isles, had I devoured. Yet the second I greeted Jonathan, it became painfully obvious to me that I lacked even the intonation of an Englishman. I realized, yet again, that I knew the grammar and the words, but I knew not the language they spoke. So I redoubled my efforts to absorb everything Jonathan had to offer.

50. The good: (Style) _____

_____

_____

And even though England didn't work out the way I had hoped, not once did anyone there suspect I was anything other than a proper Englishman going about his business in the crowded streets of mighty London, in the midst of the whirl and rush of humanity.

Through the centuries, I have always gravitated to the centers of civilization not simply to feed or prey but with a view to mastering the essential knowledge that makes each civilization dominant in its time. To be a master of all and servant to none requires a painstaking commitment to continuous learning. In ancient Greece, you'd find me in the shadows of the marketplace in the Acropolis lending a keen year to the Sophistic argumentation between Protagoras and Diogenes. In Mauryan India, I partook with King Ashoka in both the massacre at Kalinga as well as in his ensuing adoption of Buddhist tenets. How often, in the Roman Colosseum, did I smuggle in myself as a gladiator to perfect my combat skills as both the large-shielded but single greaved scutarius and also the small-shielded but double-greaved parmularius. When the YongLe Emperor decreed that the Great Wall be built in China, I immersed myself with the engineers to perfect the masonry and construction that enabled the creation of that seventh wonder of the world.[51]

51. The good: (Details) _____

_____

_____

Which brings me to the United States, the current if fleeting wonder of the modern world. It is the epicenter of exponentially proliferating knowledge, the Mecca of invention and innovation. So diverse are the options and avenues for the pursuit of mastery that my immersion in all things American will easily be my longest in any culture, past and present. I am almost in a delirium of anticipation as I consider what majors to explore in college first: shall I learn the psychotropic details of tetrahydrocannabinol in the Cannabis Chemistry major, or develop virtual cognition in the Video Gaming major, or inspect evidence from organismal and ecological perspectives in the Forensics major? Or, better yet, shall I profit from American expediency and triple-major all at once?

I will be like a kid in a candy shop on the college campus, reaching out as often as I can for a taste and a nibble to satisfy my insatiable appetite before I sink my teeth in deep to truly master the subject at hand. Only in mastery is leadership born and does conviction arise.

(689 words. Surely they keep reading beyond 650...!)

7. **Share an essay on any topic of your choice. It can be one you have already written, one that responds to a different prompt, or one of your own design.**

1.   Isn't life[52] and even living life just another form of being Un-dead? Would you[53] rather remain human and march inexorably towards death or would you rather ascend to vampire and live a life more eternal?

52. Address: (Organization) _____

_____

_____

53. The bad: _____

_____

_____

2.   It has never failed to surprise me how even the most rational of minds succumb to ignorance when it comes to the gift that I am able to bestow on humanity. People dream fondly of the elixir of eternal life, for a draught of immortality…And yet, when I present it to them, it is sheer hatred, panic, and revulsion that ensues.[54]

54. The bad: (Tone) _____

_____

_____

3.   The vampire's kiss is a liberation not a curse; it is an elevation not a fall.

4.   It has been rightly said of me that the blood of many races flows in my veins, yet it has been incorrectly assumed that the wars of violence—in which I fought as the lion fights for lordship over all—were my doing or provided cause for my exultation. Nothing can be further from the truth: I hate violence; I hate war. My actions through the millennia have been purely defensive, to protect what is mine.

5.   You could say my existence has often been swept up in whirlpools of blood, and you could also correctly say I have escaped from these not simply unscathed but invigorated and rejuvenated. Yet, I'd like to plead my innocence for any blood spilled in these incessant European wars. I'd like to claim self-defense for any manslaughter associated with my name.[55]

55. The bad: (Diction) _____

_____

_____

6.   It is no accident that after a careful survey, I chose to settle in the Carpathians and make my abode in an impregnable castle set on the highest mountain and the sheerest cliff. I expected that the sight of the dark, stone edifice perched a thousand feet up on the summit of a yawning precipice would discourage anyone from thoughts of conquest.

7.   And yet, I had discounted the irrepressible violence that bubbles like lava beneath all other elements of human nature. Far from being discouraged by my location and reputation, hordes continually assailed my kingdom. Emboldened by Thor and Wodin, the Ugrics of Iceland assaulted my domain with fell intent, not knowing that whilst they only donned the wolf headdress, I was the true werewolf and summoner of wolves. Then followed the Huns led by Attila, the fiercest of marauders who claimed that in their veins ran the blood of Scythian witches wed to the devil. After I quelled them, I can assure you the only blood that ran was Attila's in my veins. Arpad and his Hungarian Legions came knocking next, swollen with the zeal of the Honfoglalas and dreams of eastward conquest, but him too I absorbed as he lay dreaming on his back in the dark of his tent under a moonless sky. In Kosovan war, I lurked in the shadows ensuring Sultan Murad of the Ottomans defeated the Crusader army of Hunyadi if only to salvage breathing room and a modicum of rest until the next onslaught on my lands.[56]

56. The good: (Details) _____

_____

_____

8.   And come the onslaughts did. The Magyars, the Lombards, the Avar, the Bulgar, the Turk—they poured by the thousands on my frontiers and I did what I had to do to protect my lands and my vassals. But the irony of it all is that my valorous acts of self-defense have been used to paint me as a bloodthirsty, ravaging, and violent entity whereas nothing could be further from the truth.

9.   How easily humanity forgets that, left to my own devices, my conversion is selective and sensual, seductive and mutual. Far be it from me to visit violence upon my brides or my bondsmen. My embrace has a deliberate voluptuousness that my victim finds thrilling to the core. It is she who arches her back of her own volition. It is she who stretches her slender neck towards my sharp teeth shining white against blood red lips. It is she who swoons feeling my hot breath descend upon her neck. We are of equal desire when I feel her skin begin to tingle under the soft shivering touch of my lips, of equal tension as we await the release promised by the puncture of canines breaking the softest flesh. We become one in the languorous ecstasy that throbs with our eager pumping hearts.

10.   I, Count Dracula, am a lover not a fighter. And the ascension I offer is born of consummation not conflict.

(735 words. So much to say, such little space!)

CHAPTER 8
What Dracula Got Wrong (and Right)

1. **Some students have a background, identity, interest, or talent that is so meaningful that their application would be incomplete without it. If this sounds like you, then please share your story.**

> **Note:** The "or" indicates that you must choose ONE of the options listed, not ramble your way through all the options!

(Were they thinking of me, Count Dracula, when they created this prompt? I am unique in each of these categories: my background, my identity, my interest, my talent! Quite obviously my application would be incomplete without it.)

Here goes:

Unlike mere mortals[1], my consciousness doesn't begin at birth. I have always been Count Dracula. I am not of mother born nor of father seeded. My existence knows neither childhood nor aging. I am extra-racial but not extra-terrestrial (at least not to my knowledge). Popular culture considers me to be Carpathian or Romanian, Szekelian or Hungarian, Dacian or Thracian—but, I ask you, can you truly pigeonhole the ethnicity of a shape-shifting, form-changing, mutant-morphing creature of the night such as myself? I don't think so.[2]

> **1. The good:** the use of alliteration in "mere mortals."
> **1. The bad:** You sound arrogant. Remember: Ethos. Your credibility depends on being just like the reader, not superior to them.

> **2. The good:** Great writing! You have sets of 3s, and each term in the lists is balanced, showing pleasing parallel structure.

Which brings me to my unique identity. I am the original vampire[3]. While my condition has been seen as an affliction or disease or some grievous wrong against the natural order of things, I can assure you I live and breathe with the same purpose my acolyte Darwin recognized more than a century ago: survival and procreation. Though in my superhuman adaptability, the propagation of my species aka[4] vampires is advanced biology.

3. The good: Sounds like your topic is Identity.

3. The bad: This thesis should be the first sentence of your essay (if it answers the question, "What is an identity that is so meaningful...?)"

4. Address: Avoid contractions that make you sound informal. No aka's, no lol's. Spell it out: "also known as."

Yes, I am a lover and make love but the sex is just for sex's sake.[5] It is the bite—the transfusion and transmission—that creates my progeny.

5. The bad: do NOT use cliches. Cliches do not make your writing engaging.

I never give birth, but I rebirth humans into my likeness of being.

The selection of which human to elevate into my higher plane of existence relies on my innate talent[6] of being able to penetrate all the defenses that suppress true desire. Not everyone desires the exhilaration of vampiric existence. Not everyone is worthy of such elevation.

6. Address: Your story switches between the topics of IDENTITY and TALENT. Make sure you pick one topic and stick with it throughout the essay.

But those that desire me and desire what I offer wonder, "How will I ever know if I am worthy of Count Dracula's bite? And how in Satan's name will Dracula be able to find me?"

Well, fear not, needy little homo sapien.[7] My true talent, nay gift, is magnetic attraction to your innermost, deepest and darkest desires.[8] Desires you know you have, desires you are ashamed to have, and the desires you don't even know lurk deep inside.

7. The bad: Never diminish nor belittle your direct audience (in this case, the admissions committee!).

8. The bad: Avoid negative diction: "darkest desires" gives a sinister twist to the narration of your talent.

But I, Count Dracula, know your darkest desires! I feel them! I am drawn to them! It is your desire I feast on as I suck your blood! And if the rapture of our commingling is worthy enough, you are in! you are transfigured into my likeness and join my legion.[9]

9. The bad: Avoid using the second person address: "you." Use the third person address (desires "one" has or desires "they" have).

In all honesty, I consider this talent to be my greatest gift.

(375 words...too short. I don't know what else to write.)

Additional Commentary by DVS:

Overall, the essay lacks focus and purpose. Clearly, the goal here is to convince the target audience that you are worthy of admission. However, the journey you take us on clearly shows that the devil, in this case, is literally in the details…!

No one in their sane minds would admit you onto their campus should they read phrases such as "…I suck your blood," and "needy little homo sapien" !

Your attention is also clearly split between writing a story about your IDENTITY or about your TALENT. You must choose one and elaborate on it with details that do not alienate your reader.

Finally, your essay lacks structure. Please be mindful of the challenge you face in these 650 words: Tell us how your life shaped you to become who you are but also who you want to become as you embark on your life-changing college experience.

Portions of this essay are well-written and might be incorporated into the rewrite.

2. **The lessons we take from obstacles we encounter can be fundamental to later success. Recount a time when you faced a challenge, setback, or failure. How did it affect you, and what did you learn from the experience?**

From the countless campaigns I waged over the centuries—as King and Commander in the Dark Ages, as Count and C.E.O in the Modern Ages—the setback that makes me most rueful is a fleeting episode in the saga of my somnambulist conquests. In England, in 1899, I identified nothing less than a woman worthy of ascension to Queen of the Undead.[10] Her name was Mina Harker. Her pent up desires overwhelmed me with their unabashed embrace of the forbidden.[11]

> **10. The bad:** Word Choice/Diction: If it is "fleeting" why write about it? Instead of somnambulist "conquests," try "somnambulist sorties." Why "Queen of the Undead," why not, "Queen of the Vampires"?

> **11. The bad:** Too overtly sexual. (Dracula, you're applying to be on a campus full of young co-eds!). Delete.

My very first glimpse of Mina, and I realized why London had been calling me all along, why I had endured passage in choppy seas, why I had acquired properties all across that grimy city, why[12] I had been putting myself out of my comfort zone by sleeping in rudimentary boxes filled with my native soil. Here she was, my wondrous Wilhelmina, kin of my kin, yearning for the liberation that only my teeth sunk deep into her neck[13] could deliver.

> **12. The bad:** insert "and" before the last "why" to create a compound sentence structure.

> **13. The good:** vivid imagery that uses the five senses (touch, taste, sight, sound, and smell).
> **13. The bad:** Ouch! Too gory, my bloodsucking friend. Try: "that only my enchanting incision on the hollow of her neck could deliver."

But to get to Mina, to indoctrinate and to assimilate[14] Mina, to absorb Mina and to transform her into becoming the queen of my coterie of undead countesses proved to be an abject failure.

> **14. The bad:** Word Choice/Diction: avoid "Indoctrinate" and "assimilate" when used as actions on humans.

My objectives were constantly thwarted by a bunch of do-gooders led by the nefarious Dr. Van Helsing, the luckiest devil to ever have crossed my path and survived.[15] At me he thrust garlic, at me he brandished The Cross, at me he tossed sacramental wafers, and guess what?[16] Because he found me repulsed, he thought his religion had power over me!

15. Address: Putting down Van Helsing as a "lucky devil" belittles your adversary. Try instead: "...Van Helsing, the canniest adversary to ever have crossed my path."

16. The bad: TONE: avoid a chatty, informal tone.

If only Helsing knew that I was affected not by any mystical force of his moronic[17] charms but because of allergens! Brandish me your crucifix today, Van Helsing, and I'll brandish you my Epipen.

17. The bad: Word Choice/Diction: Try instead, "superstitious charms."

But I digress. Truth be told, even today I tip my hat to the resolve of the Stoker gang for making that concerted effort that thwarted my conquest of Mina.

They burst upon me during that primal moment when I had Mina entranced, ensconced in my bosom, and suckling the very life blood from the freshly incised artery in my chest. I was in a rapture, a delight swelling up in me that would surely explode to fill up the universe itself.[18]

18. The good: graphic imagery using the five senses.
18. The bad: Too raunchy, too sexually charged for an admissions committee.

Mina had succumbed, her barriers had dissipated, and she was eager to merge. Perhaps I let my guard down, perhaps I lingered too long in the bliss of this Vampire baptism. Perhaps I fell prey to my own overconfidence, but I failed to hear them until it was too late.

To my dismay, they were armed with all of the aforementioned allergens that debilitate me. I got so furious at the interruption of my bodacious banquet that I couldn't think straight and barely curbed my involuntary reaction of pouncing on the gang to tear them to shreds.

But sanity prevailed and I made my exit. At the time, I was rather sanguine about finding Mina and having her all to myself in the near future.

How wrong I was!

They worked in concert to infiltrate and booby trap all my coffin-boxes around London—in Carfax, Bermondsey, Mile End, Walworth. The men even had the temerity to lay an ambush for me at my abode in Piccadilly, armed as always with those god-forsaken allergens hidden in their crucifixes and wafers. Long story short, I was chased out of London and stalked all the way to my home in Transylvania. And Mina, I was never able to deliver the poor soul from her mortal existence, never able to give her what she truly desired—becoming Queen of the Undead and ruling by my side.

This failure affected me deeply. Despite my superior being, I was thwarted by mere mortals. I took the defeat to heart (no pun intended) and conducted a clinical analysis of why I had failed in my conquest of Mina and, more importantly, how I would never fail again in my future endeavors.

After much reflection, I realized that my enterprise suffered from inadequate preparation, planning, and execution in four domains: delegation, anticipation, underestimation, and, last but not least, medication.[19]

19. The good: STRUCTURE: Excellent transition and well laid out logical structure.

Delegation. I had gone solo. Never again. Granted, I am invincible; yet, I cannot be at multiple places at once. When faced by an enemy united in their numbers and coordinated in their actions, I cannot outmaneuver them by myself. For my expedition to London, I should have conscripted the services of the Three Sisters instead of leaving them behind to toy with Jonathan Harker. I should have used that profligate lunatic Renfield to greater advantage instead of too soon snapping his neck. I should have created my own little army of progeny to command and marshall in the field, disposing of them[20] once they'd performed their duties.

20. The bad: Word Choice/Diction: Instead of "...disposing of them..." try instead, "...liberating them..."

Anticipation. Sure, I was strategic in my plans, from the purchase of properties in prime locations, to shipping more than adequate supplies of native-soil coffins, to preying on my chosen women at the most opportune times. However, I paid scant regard to the possibility that my foes, though weaklings in most regards, were equally endowed with strategic acumen. While they anticipated my every move, I failed to examine their countermoves—they were playing chess not checkers. It was a humbling realization. From that moment forward, I always put myself in my adversaries' shoes before deciding on my next course of action.

Underestimation: I believed my adversary, the Stoker gang, to be weak just because they seemed to rely too much on religious icons. I was too quick to peg them with the religious fanatics I'd been encountering for centuries, people wed to superstition and dying for divine intervention. But Drs. Van Helsing, Seward et al. turned out to be confounding creatures whose swiftness for scientific experimentation was instrumental in defeating me. They figured out that the soil in my coffin had nutrients essential to my regeneration. They almost saved Lucy by administering blood transfusions. They collated multiple records of their interactions with me in order to analyze my predatory habits and create plans based on cold, hard logic. They exploited my telepathic bond with Mina. Underestimating their scientific acumen cost me victory. After London, I resolved: Never again.

Medication: if only they'd invented the epipen in 1899 instead of 1987. I go nowhere without it now. Come at me, crucifix! Whatchoo got, garlic?! Watch out, wafers! [21] I have privately funded the development of multidose autoinjectors (yes, yes, patent violations and all that)[22] and I never leave home without it. You could say that the epipen is the only gun I'll ever need to carry into a battle and Epinephrine is my silver bullet.

21. The good: Well done! Humor is always welcome.

22. The bad: DETAILS: Unnecessary detail. Delete.

(1102 words! Too long. I don't know what to cut…)

Additional Commentary by DVS:

1. **Organization:** While this essay has great organization the second part, at the onset it meanders through details that seem irrelevant to addressing the topic. For a revision, throw your reader into the story of how the Van Helsing Gang interrupted your communion with Mina Harker. Begin with "Even today I tip my hat to the resolve of the Stoker Gang…"

2. **Purpose:** you seem too quick to inject sexual and/or gory details and sentiments in your writing. Remember: your essay must convince your target audience, the admissions committee, that you are worthy of inclusion on their campus made up of bright, young, and innocent young adults. Straying into the darker aspects of your vampiric existence or sharing with unabashed glee the overpowering sexuality of your encounters will not gain you any admission points. Quite the contrary, it will make the admissions committee want to ward off their campus with garlic and crucifixes against you.

3. **Word Choice (WC)/Diction:** a recurring error in your writing is negative diction. Words with negative connotations influence the reader in negative ways. While I have pointed out a host of these in my comments, let me draw your attention to some of the diction that works against you: "indoctrinate," "Devil," "nefarious," "moronic," "enemy," "disposing," "preying," "weaklings," "weak," "creatures," "predatory." Piling on a list of negative words in your college essay—it has the inevitable effect of creating a negative impression about you, the writer.

4. **Optics:** every story has its details but it is how you show those details that matter. you are not telling the truth as it happened but couching the truth in a manner that is beneficial to your purpose of gaining admission to the college of your choice.

3. Reflect on a time when you questioned or challenged a belief or idea. What prompted your thinking? What was the outcome?

From the very onset of my existence,[23] I have challenged the notion of binary sex and sexuality. Mine is a creative biology that literally transforms the site of desire from the conventional erogenous zones (genitalia, for most of you mortals) to those twin orifices on the neck: delicious, blood-tinged, and pulsing for more.

> **23. The bad:** False Claim: surely not from the very onset! Instead say: "As far back as I can remember…"

The world regards my conquests as victims, but they could not be more wrong! Properly speaking, both my "victim" and I are submissive partners, submitting[24] to each other in turns. The blood I drink from your neck, the blood you drink from my bosom[25]—a cycle of orgiastic becoming.

> **24. The bad:** Word choice/Diction: submissive & submit are repetitive: try instead, "…consenting partners, submitting…"

> **25. The bad:** Word Choice/Diction: instead of "blood I drink" use "elixir I imbibe, etcetera."

In my lovemaking, I am always subverting the heterodoxy of sexuality, turning on its head the belief system that males are males and females are females. I am the sole progenitor: I am both mother and father, father and mother; both husband and wife, and wife and husband. All my hordes[26] are procreated from me and me alone.

> **26. The bad:** Word Choice/Diction: "hordes" is a pejorative, a word with negative connotations. Try instead: "All my lineage is procreated…"

People believe that bloodlust is what makes us vampire. They couldn't be further from the truth. What makes us vampires is the act of disrobing the garments imposed by society. Humans tend to wear the clothes chosen for them from the time of birth to the time of death: male to be blue to be boy, female to be pink to be girl.[27]

> **27. The good:** STYLE: Great use of metaphor and parallelism. Well done!

To be vampire is to be black to be more.[28]

> **28. The good:** Excellent use of the dramatic one-sentence paragraph. Well done!

To be vampire is to be a being without binary.

I wouldn't stir up a fuss about this except for the fuss stirred up by your kind, the males amongst the mortals. So much effort is expended in all parts of the world to hide the fact that the limitations of the roles males can play—and the roles females cannot play—is based on nothing more than arbitrary destiny.[29]

One might say that I have chafed at this global conspiracy to keep men up and women down—for centuries I have played the role of liberator, turning women to my cause.

I submit, with a sense of understated humility, that I, Count Dracula, am the first feminist.

So the question becomes: what has been the outcome of my concerted efforts at undermining and exposing male complicity in the global oppression of others?

Clearly, I have been demonized by the male world. Theirs has been an unflagging smear-campaign fueled by the deep seated resentment of (male) power brokers around the planet. Their world might be divided in its representations of the devil as a tempting and sinful agent, but it is united in its portrayal of Dracula as a malevolent and unnatural beast.

Yet, there has been another outcome, a transformative change in society for which I am responsible but for which I will forever remain its unsung hero. I speak of the inexorable shift away from the oppression of patriarchy through the centuries.

Were it not for my late night jaunts across the world and into the bedchambers of the powerful, the world would not be in the state of gender liberation that it is today. The amount of research, planning, and execution I have undertaken in terms of identifying the best placed victims for vampiric conversion merits a Nobel Prize in Physiology or Medicine, perhaps even in Economics.[30]

I have taken the best of the best females to the next level of biology and reduced the most vainglorious of men to compliance.[31]

So many wars have I averted by a pointed nibble, simple possession and quick conversion of the right person at the right place and the right time.

This makes me wonder: why not the Nobel Peace Prize for Count Dracula?

(592 words. Getting there!)

Additional Commentary by DVS:

Style: Overall, this essay has many fine qualities. There is an engaging style in the writing and the subject matter (challenging binary sex and sexuality, going against the heterodoxy of patriarchal society) is current and would gain you traction with any admissions committee. Well done!

Off Topic: As noted, there are moments in this essay that your enthusiasm takes you off course. Remember: It is really important to keep a laser focus on your chosen topic and then use it to convince the audience/admissions committee why what you are sharing makes you worthy of admission to their campus.

So What?: The flaw of this essay—and it is a significant one—is that it doesn't offer any clear picture of how your experience with binary sex and sexuality will translate to meaningful contributions on the college campus. In other words, you claim that you challenged patriarchy and helped women's liberation. Assuming the reader buys this, you still have to answer, so how will this experience make you contribute what to the college campus?

Tone: The voice in this essay much too often sounds overly pompous and self-conceited. Your rewrite must build in room for humility, questioning, wonder—essential attributes for any college applicant.

Optics: While on the one hand you want to stay true to the depiction and description of your Vampiric being and experiences, it is important to couch the truth in a manner that does not automatically alienate your reader.

4. **Reflect on something that someone has done for you that has made you happy or thankful in a surprising way. How has this gratitude affected or motivated you?**

Lucy Westenra.[32]

32. The good: STYLE: dramatic start! Those of us familiar with your chronicles know of Lucy W. You've grabbed your reader's attention!

If I might be allowed to claim that Mina Harker was my first experience of love at first sight, then I would like to aver that meeting Lucy in her unguarded somnambulance surprised me with a happiness I hadn't thought possible.

I will never cease to be grateful for what snowy Lucy in her white nightdress gave me that night in the ruins of St. Mary's Church. Little did I know—as I lurked behind her bench watching the rays of the full moon slide down her exposed skin—that it was I who was about to be ravished.

What Lucy gave to me was the realization that there is always something new and unknown waiting to be discovered no matter how jaded by immortality you[33] might be. Excuse me—how jaded by immortality I might be.

33. The bad: Word Choice/Diction: avoid the 2nd-person pronoun: instead of "you," use "one."

After all, when you have lived as long as I have, you have pretty much done it all, experienced it all. Believe it or not, being eternal has its drawbacks—not least of which is the fact that one is hard-pressed to find any truly new, undiscovered, and unexpected pleasure in this monotony called walking dead.[34]

34. The bad: PURPOSE: Off-topic: delete. If this is true, then any reader in the admissions committee would wonder why you need college to begin with..!

For how long had I been yearning to be yanked from the repetition of the same, and how unexpected was finding a novel intoxication in Lucy's embrace.

Simply put: I had never clasped any of my tender targets, never first sunk my eager canines into the soft curve of exposed neck whilst they were in that mysterious state of simultaneous consciousness and unconsciousness: the sleepwalker's drift.

You see, I had no idea that Lucy was in sleep-walking condition[35] when she arched her back to gaze at the moon, stretched out her arms to clasp me by the neck, and drew me down from behind the bench for my first taste of her.[36]

35. The bad: WORDY: instead of "Lucy was in sleep-walking condition," say: "Lucy was sleepwalking."

36. The bad: Word Choice/Diction: Instead of "drew me down...for my first taste of her," say: "drew me down...for my first crimson kiss."

And how unexpectedly explosive the experience was! All the frustrations of my seaborne journey on that cursed ship Demeter, all the tension of my novel venture in that undiscovered country called England, all my perpetual watchful wariness of being a stranger in a strange land—all of it dissolved into an ecstasy of unbidden fireworks to rival the merriment of the dancing stars in the night sky above us. I became a mindless, powerless entity as her blood pulsed in my mouth, losing all reserve and all caution, wanting this moment to last forever, wanting to howl at the moon for eternity.[37]

37. The good: IMAGERY: Great Writing: well done! it conveys the unexpected power of your encounter through the use of vivid details.

And how full of delight was the process of somnambulist conversion! Heretofore, I had been using the mesmeric power of my glowing eyes to entrance my victims, to make them swoon with unbidden desire for my suck. But Lucy's blood,[38] as it pulsed its way down my throat, had me entranced with a whole host of sensations I hadn't known existed. The ecstasy was beyond belief. I lost all sense of time and space. I was floating in pure delight.

38. The bad: Word Choice/Diction: Instead of "victims," say: "companions"; instead of "my suck," say: "my special caress"; instead of "Lucy's blood," say: "Lucy's essence."

Only to be interrupted by Mina Harker!

Despite my raging fury at the untimely disruption, I held back from attacking Mina. Because, you see, I was working out how to relive my titillating tryst with Lucy. Ah, dear admissions committee, I wanted Lucy again and again and again. She had become my dependency.[39]

39. The bad: avoid the language of addiction.

The only question I kept asking myself was: how to prolong my carnal cavort[40] with sleepwalking Lucy without completely converting her into a vampire?

40. The bad: Word Choice/Diction: Too much information! avoid sexual language. Instead of "my carnal cavort," say: "our impassioned and mutual embrace."

Well, fortune was on my side. It was my very enemies led by Van Helsing who unwittingly ensured that Lucy would be replenished after our trysts to sleepwalk yet another night! In their zeal to revive her, they daily administered blood transfusions not knowing that they were merely replenishing her for our nighttime affairs.

And yet, all things human come to end. When Lucy crossed over and even before she was executed in cold blood by the Helsing group, I made a solemn promise: to do everything in my power to research the science behind somnambulist conversion.[41]

41. Address: This is the only time that you address the 2nd part of the prompt: how has this gratitude affected or motivated you? What kind of research have you carried out into the science of somnambulism? With what results?

For this unexpected and novel ecstasy, I will forever be grateful to you, my sweet sleepwalking Lucy.

(670 words. Practice makes perfect!)

Additional Commentary by DVS:

Address the prompt: while you are successful in depicting the unexpected emotional impact of your encounter with Lucy Westenra, you fail to address the second part of the prompt: how has the gratitude motivated you? This second part is the more important one to address: this is the opportunity to tell the admissions committee about some of the pursuits and research that might tip the scales in your favor.

Style: There are segments here that are beautifully crafted. Well done!

Optics: As usual, be mindful of couching the truth in a manner that does not lead to automatic alienation or rejection on the part of your reader. I acknowledge that you must speak truthfully about who you are and what you do as Count Dracula; however, you have to acknowledge that you need to make some accommodations in your Word Choice/Diction in order to maximize your chances of admission.

Remember: the question being asked, at all times, is: "what can you tell me in this essay that would convince me that you belong on my amazing campus teeming with all the previously admitted amazing students?" Play the game, Dracula, play the game!

5. Discuss an accomplishment, event, or realization that sparked a period of personal growth and a new understanding of yourself or others.

Albert, one of my favorite conversions, is often quoted for saying something that I personally told him when regaling him with tales from my days at the Scholomance in Romania. "Great spirits have always encountered violent opposition from mediocre minds." I came up with that quote first—you can ask him yourself if you find him, but he'll probably tell you it is all relative.[42]

42. The good: Humor: the allusion to Einstein is noted.

There are many books written about my origins and most of them get it wrong. One thing they don't get right enough, however, is the fact that The Dark Arts & Magic School near Hermannstadt, the fabled Scholomance, was indeed everything superstitious Romanians believed it to be and then some.

To be fair to the Romanian villagers and the wandering gypsies, the latter of whom I considered to be my vassals, the fact that a dark magic war was waged between the Scholomance wizard and me for years across the countryside must have been the cause for the plethora of local superstitions in the first place. We fought battles in the dark recesses of the forests, mountains, and caves as we sought each other's annihilation. And, as you might expect, it is the victor's name that lurks behind every superstitious fear: *Gregynia Drakuluj* (Devil's garden), *Gania Drakuluj* (Devil's mountain), *Yadu Drakuluj* (Devil's abyss).

The antagonism between Feurix and myself only arose because of rank jealousy on his part. At the start of my apprenticeship, Feurix embraced and quickly elevated me to the rank of Tenth, the Dragonrider—he who would awaken the beast from the depths of the lake and ride him to cast thunderstorms far and wide. But, given my preternatural talents as *nosferatu*, he became envious of my easy mastery. Whereas Feurix knew all the secrets of nature, the language of animals, and the alchemy of compounds, he became ever more recalcitrant in imparting their inner workings to me.

I hadn't realized that grudging envy had transformed into vengeful fury when an exercise in necromantic regeneration using the blackest of soul gems turned out to be a deathly booby trap. Feurix had already animated the mummified corpse with a warrior spirit, so that when I sliced open the restraining bands, I found myself under the onslaught of a scimitar wielding demon. I barely escaped thanks to my ingenuity and supernatural reflexes.

Thereafter, it was open warfare. I was determined to stamp out Feurix.[43] Our conflict waged over days and weeks. One day, I'll give the world a step-by-step account of how I defeated the wily, cunning, and masterful Feurix in a book I'd like to entitle *The Full Blood Prince and the Deathly Grotto*.[44] Suffice it to say that it was only when I had won that I realized what I had lost.

43. The bad: Word Choice/Diction: Instead of "to stamp out" try: "to neutralize..."

I had lost access to the vast knowledge Feurix possessed in the dark and arcane arts. In the shortest of times, he had taught me things that are the stuff of legend today: how to[45] throw neither shadow nor mirror reflection; how to summon elemental power for superhuman strength; how to transform into wolf, dog, bat, and even dust; how to create a mist to shroud my seaward journeys; how to dematerialize to slip through a hairbreadth of space; how to see in the blackest of nights.

But, had I been longer favored with his tutelage, I would have learnt to overcome my glaring limitations. Even today, my power ceases at the coming of the day. Even today,[46] I cannot enter without someone bidding me in. Even today, I must replenish by resting in the soil of my ancestral home; even today, I cannot swim in any form of natural water—be it ocean, river, or lake; Even today, I am helpless as a newborn as I lie in my coffin.

As the years pass, I've come to understand that something is always lost for something gained. Feurix could have taught me so much more had he lived; and yet, his death had become inevitable given his limitations and jealousy. His was a mediocre mind that violently opposed me; mine was the soaring spirit that got prematurely clipped.[47]

(681 words)

Additional Commentary by DVS:

Organization: As noted, your paragraphs and the information they contain need to be resequenced. Be mindful that the essay requires a 2-part response: the event and the effects of that event. You have unusual and very unique source material here: school of magic, supernatural spells, dragons, etc. However, you need to do justice to your source by putting the reader in the moment first and reflecting on what you learned second. Don't panic—once you go through the essayt.com workshop, you will have a full understanding of what this rewrite entails.

Style: As noted, a good portion of this essay is stylistically pleasing and well written. Well done!

Purpose: While the subject matter is engaging, your story lacks the punchline or the "so what?" aspect that tells the admissions committee why this experience makes you stand out as a college candidate, or indeed how this experience has shaped the horizon of your expectations for the near future. In other words, you learned that mediocre minds will try to clip the wings of your soaring spirit (to use your own words), but how does this lesson make you worthy of college admissions? Let us discuss when we conference.

6. Describe a topic, idea, or concept you find so engaging that it makes you lose all track of time. Why does it captivate you? What or who do you turn to when you want to learn more?

Mastery.

I have so lived my eternal life, so conceived of all my actions, so as to be Master. In subservience is failure. In mastery is overcoming. In my heart of hearts, I have desired nothing more than becoming the Master of all humanity in order to snatch them out of their lives of self-inflicted violence and suffering and transmute them into a likeness of my being.[48]

48. Address: TONE: Ouch! Dracula: while the motive may be noble (the end of violence and suffering), couching it in the language of mastery over humanity is going to scare every reader and lead to an immediate rejection of your application. Try instead: "My search for mastery has been motivated by the search of a solution to ending the self-inflicted violence and suffering that plagues humanity."

Becoming the Master is an infinitely consuming task. Thankfully, I Count Dracula have infinite time on hand. But when time stretches out like an endless scroll, it becomes easy, much too easy, to lose track of it.[49] In my life as a Boyar, I became master to the Peasants and also the Szigane; yet I would be remiss if I didn't share the fact that I spent a couple of centuries achieving what could have taken mere dec ades simply because time is never of the essence for me.

49. The bad: MIXED METAPHOR: If time is an endless scroll, why would you "lose track of it"? Instead try: "...when time stretches out like an endless scroll, it becomes easy...to get lost in the minutiae of detail."

Or take my misfortunate foray into England more than a century ago. Prior to orchestrating the arrival of Jonathan Harker to my castle in Transylvania, I had lost myself for decades in the study of everything British. I had mastered the language, the customs, and the idioms. Each and every book on the subject of England that I could lay my hands on, had I devoured.[50] Each and every guest hailing from the British Isles, had I devoured. Yet the second I greeted Jonathan, it became painfully obvious to me that I lacked even the intonation of an Englishman. I realized, yet again, that I knew the grammar and the words, but I knew not the language they spoke. So I redoubled my efforts to absorb everything Jonathan had to offer.

50. The good: STYLE: nice use of the repetition of the phrase at the end of your sentences (epistrophe) for dramatic effect. Well done!

And even though England didn't work out the way I had hoped, not once did anyone there suspect I was anything other than a proper Englishman going about his business in the crowded streets of mighty London, in the midst of the whirl and rush of humanity.

Through the centuries, I have always gravitated to the centers of civilization not simply to feed or prey but with a view to mastering the essential knowledge that makes each civilization dominant in its time. To be a master of all and servant to none requires a painstaking commitment to continuous learning. In ancient Greece, you'd find me in the shadows of the marketplace in the Acropolis lending a keen year to the Sophistic argumentation between Protagoras and Diogenes. In Mauryan India, I partook with King Ashoka in both the massacre at Kalinga as well as in his ensuing adoption of Buddhist tenets. How often, in the Roman Colosseum, did I smuggle in myself as a gladiator to perfect my combat skills as both the large-shielded but single greaved scutarius and also the small-shielded but double-greaved parmularius. When the YongLe Emperor decreed that the Great Wall be built in China, I immersed myself with the engineers to perfect the masonry and construction that enabled the creation of that seventh wonder of the world.[51]

51. The good: DETAILS: excellent use of specific details. This list lends credibility to your story.

Which brings me to the United States, the current if fleeting wonder of the modern world. It is the epicenter of exponentially proliferating knowledge, the Mecca of invention and innovation. So diverse are the options and avenues for the pursuit of mastery that my immersion in all things American will easily be my longest in any culture, past and present. I am almost in a delirium of anticipation as I consider what majors to explore in college first: shall I learn the psychotropic details of tetrahydrocannabinol in the Cannabis Chemistry major, or develop virtual cognition in the Video Gaming major, or inspect evidence from organismal and ecological perspectives in the Forensics major? Or, better yet, shall I profit from American expediency and triple-major all at once?

I will be like a kid in a candy shop on the college campus, reaching out as often as I can for a taste and a nibble to satisfy my insatiable appetite before I sink my teeth in deep to truly master the subject at hand. Only in mastery is leadership born and does conviction arise.

(688 words. Surely they keep reading beyond 650…!)

Additional Commentary by DVS:

The Prompt: Note here that the prompt breaks down into three distinct parts. While you have done a great job of answering the first two parts (what concept do you find so engaging and why does it captivate you?), you really haven't reflected on the third part (whom do you turn to?). It is implied through your list of details that you learn from expert practitioners of their respective crafts. You should make this explicit as also relate it to your desire to learn from "master practitioners" in college, namely professors with PhDs who also spearhead the latest research in various domains of knowledge. Here, you might have an opportunity to tailor the "latest research" to each college in specific based on what their professors specialize in.

Style: overall, assuming you wrote these essays sequentially, your writing is becoming more powerful in both content and style. This essay is rich with details that showcase the vast array of your experiences. Well done!

Ethos: Do not alienate your reader as you do in the first paragraph by claiming to desire "becoming the Master of all humanity"! This is a running concern in all your essays so far: you fail to create a persona that shows a connection with the reader. The I-am-just-like-you and We-are-all-in-this-together is essential for your admissions committee reader to engage sympathetically with what you have to say—as opposed to being frightened by what you are capable of as Prince of Darkness!

7. **Share an essay on any topic of your choice. It can be one you have already written, one that responds to a different prompt, or one of your own design.**

1. Isn't life[52] and even living life just another form of being Un-dead? Would you[53] rather remain human and march inexorably towards death or would you rather ascend to vampire and live a life more eternal?

52. The bad: ORGANIZATION: The sequencing in this essay should be re-ordered as follows: Paragraphs 4, 6, 7, 8, 9 10, 3, 1. Delete: paragraphs 2 & 5. (see additional notes for explanation).

53. The bad: ADDRESS: Avoid the use of the second person pronoun "you."

2. It has never failed to surprise me how even the most rational of minds succumb to ignorance when it comes to the gift that I am able to bestow on humanity. People dream fondly of the elixir of eternal life, for a draught of immortality…And yet, when I present it to them, it is sheer hatred, panic, and revulsion that ensues.[54]

54. The bad: TONE: Delete entire paragraph: it is pompous (gift that I…bestow on humanity); also, it employs negative diction (hatred, panic, revulsion).

3. The vampire's kiss is a liberation not a curse; it is an elevation not a fall.

4. It has been rightly said of me that the blood of many races flows in my veins, yet it has been incorrectly assumed that the wars of violence—in which I fought as the lion fights for lordship over all—were my doing or provided cause for my exultation. Nothing can be further from the truth: I hate violence; I hate war. My actions through the millennia have been purely defensive, to protect what is mine.

5. You could say my existence has often been swept up in whirlpools of blood, and you could also correctly say I have escaped from these not simply unscathed but invigorated and rejuvenated. Yet, I'd like to plead my innocence for any blood spilled in these incessant European wars. I'd like to claim self-defense for any manslaughter associated with my name.[55]

55. The bad: Word Choice/Diction: You utilize the diction of criminality ("blood spilled," "manslaughter," "self-defense"). Also, the information is repetitive. Delete the entire paragraph!

6.   It is no accident that after a careful survey, I chose to settle in the Carpathians and make my abode in an impregnable castle set on the highest mountain and the sheerest cliff. I expected that the sight of the dark, stone edifice perched a thousand feet up on the summit of a yawning precipice would discourage anyone from thoughts of conquest.

7.   And yet, I had discounted the irrepressible violence that bubbles like lava beneath all other elements of human nature. Far from being discouraged by my location and reputation, hordes continually assailed my kingdom. Emboldened by Thor and Wodin, the Ugrics of Iceland assaulted my domain with fell intent, not knowing that whilst they only donned the wolf headdress, I was the true werewolf and summoner of wolves. Then followed the Huns led by Attila, the fiercest of marauders who claimed that in their veins ran the blood of Scythian witches wed to the devil. After I quelled them, I can assure you the only blood that ran was Attila's in my veins. Arpad and his Hungarian Legions came knocking next, swollen with the zeal of the Honfoglalas and dreams of eastward conquest, but him too I absorbed as he lay dreaming on his back in the dark of his tent under a moonless sky. In Kosovan war, I lurked in the shadows ensuring Sultan Murad of the Ottomans defeated the Crusader army of Hunyadi if only to salvage breathing room and a modicum of rest until the next onslaught on my lands.[56]

> **56. The good:** DETAILS: Excellent use of details to create specificity in representing the breadth and scope of your experience. Well done!

8.   And come the onslaughts did. The Magyars, the Lombards, the Avar, the Bulgar, the Turk—they poured by the thousands on my frontiers and I did what I had to do to protect my lands and my vassals. But the irony of it all is that my valorous acts of self-defense have been used to paint me as a bloodthirsty, ravaging, and violent entity whereas nothing could be further from the truth.

9.   How easily humanity forgets that, left to my own devices, my conversion is selective and sensual, seductive and mutual. Far be it from me to visit violence upon my brides or my bondsmen. My embrace has a deliberate voluptuousness that my victim finds thrilling to the core. It is she who arches her back of her own volition. It is she who stretches her slender neck towards my sharp teeth shining white against blood red lips. It is she who swoons feeling my hot breath descend upon her neck. We are of equal desire when I feel her skin begin to tingle under the soft shivering touch of my lips, of equal tension as we await the release promised by the puncture of canines breaking the softest flesh. We become one in the languorous ecstasy that throbs with our eager pumping hearts.

10.   I, Count Dracula, am a lover not a fighter. And the ascension I offer is born of consummation not conflict.

(735 words. So much to say, such little space!)

Additional Commentary by DVS:

Organization: This essay attempts to clear a major misunderstanding propagated in history and culture about your Vampire existence, namely the fact that you abhor violence. As noted above, your paragraphs should be resequenced as follows:

Paragraph 4: introduce the main topic: "I hate violence. I hate war."

Paragraph 6: you chose to settle in a remote location to avoid conflict.

Paragraphs 7 & 8: violence visited to you by bloodthirsty hordes over the centuries.

Paragraph 9, 10, & 3: transition into your true calling: conversion through seduction, not violence.

Paragraph 1: Open ended questions to leave the reader food for thought.

Writing Quality: Your writing is rich with details and specifics and shows your broad range of experience with different races, cultures, and nationalities through the course of your existence. The prose is fluid and engaging. Well done!

CHAPTER 9
Essential Elements of Style in Writing

When I discuss The College Essay with students in the 11th- and 12th-grades, I discover that no one paid attention in English class. A common refrain I hear is that English classes don't teach you how to write this all-important, life-changing document.

This is a false claim.

Let us recall for a brief moment the reasons why we study Literature in the English classroom:

We study Literature to immerse ourselves in stories that inhabit worlds whose quirks and complexities, elations and adversities mirror our very own world, the real world.

We study Literature to befriend protagonists who are launched into journeys full of adventures and misadventures, and with them we discover profound truths hidden in the mystery of our existence.

Above all, we study Literature for entertainment because we yearn to witness how the hero negotiates conflict, how the hero falls but also rises, and how the hero overcomes the particulars of their life to arrive at the universals of all our lives.

If you think about it, the reason we love to read Literature is very much the reason colleges ask you to craft The College Essay which is properly speaking "A Story of Your Journey So Far."

The College Essay is an invitation to share the particulars of your own journey through life.

As a young adult, you have a dawning realization of your personal quest. And this quest is shaped by everything you have experienced and everything you have chosen to do (and not do).

From the particulars of your choices and from the particulars of your own experiences, there emerges a unique being that is you and only you and no one else. And yet, when you share your story in all its heroic specificity, you tap into universal truths that all of us can recognize because they are also our truths.

So yes, your English class has always prepared you to write The College Essay as "The Story of My Journey So Far."

Think for a second of someone who tells a good story. They entertain you, they make you laugh, they make you cry. The same story told by another person falls flat. You can tell the same story in a way that has your audience hanging on to your next word or has them checking the exits.

Why is that? Because it is not so much what you're telling (content) but how you're telling it (form). **A great story needs form as well as content.** And since you are writing your story, you need to have a grasp on some essential elements of style in writing (form) so that you can best convey the amazing journey of your life so far (content).

While the elements of style are aplenty, I would encourage you to familiarize yourself with the shortlist provided below.

Try to incorporate some of these basics in your writing, and I guarantee you that your story will read all the better for it. (Not to mention all your college writing as well as professional writing in the future!)

Crash course: Elements of Style

By now you have come to realize that The College Essay is a 650 word story that highlights the journey of your life so far.

What moments from your journey should you include in this story? And, equally important, how should you tell this story?

The answer to both questions is to be found in the word **persuasion**. After all, you are writing the story of your journey in life to persuade the admissions committee that you are a worthy candidate, to persuade them that you belong on their campus.

Luckily for us, a philosopher from ancient Greece named Aristotle spent quite a bit of his time thinking about the art of persuasion. In fact, he wrote an entire book on the subject of persuasion: On Rhetoric.

And while one might not think of storytelling through the lens of rhetoric (which is applied to dissect speeches in the political arena), for our purpose—to persuade the admissions committee—a discussion of style must begin with the three "persuaders" identified by Aristotle.

1. The three persuaders: Ethos, Pathos, and Logos

Ethos: Persuasion produced through the character of the storyteller.

Why should I believe anything you say? What is your credibility? Are you knowledgeable in the topic? Do you speak out of experience or hearsay?

Equally important here are the following questions: Are you someone like me? Are we in this together? Are you the type of person I can vibe with and connect with?

Pathos: Persuasion produced through the emotional state of the audience.

If you fail to arouse an emotional reaction in your audience, if your story leaves them cold, it is very unlikely you will have succeeded in persuading them. You must make your audience feel for you, for your cause, and feel the importance of your message.

Regardless of the story you are telling, its ultimate message is "Admit me! Admit me!"

Logos: persuasion produced through the reasoning behind the argument.

Because you are writing this story to gain admissions into the dream college you have always wanted to attend, and because you want them to have no doubt on their decision making, you need to convince them with facts, reasoning, and logic.

Ethos, Pathos, Logos

Weak:

I am the type of applicant that will enhance the campus experience for all involved because I have an outgoing personality, believe in helping others, delegate or follow as the situation demands, and want to make the world a better place. (lacks personality)

Pathos as persuader:

Imagine the positive ripple effect I could have on your campus. My outgoing personality would spark new friendships, and my passion for helping others would create a more supportive environment. I'm a team player, happy to delegate or take charge depending on the need. Deep down, I believe we all share the desire to make a difference, and at your college, I could contribute to a community that strives to do just that.

Ethos as persuader:

My dedication to fostering a positive campus environment is rooted in both my outgoing personality and strong work ethic. I thrive in collaborative settings, adept at delegating tasks for efficiency and seamlessly following directions when needed. This adaptability, coupled with my genuine desire to help others, makes me a valuable asset to any team. My commitment to making a positive impact extends beyond the classroom; I actively seek opportunities to contribute to a better world.

Logos as persuader:

My outgoing personality fosters inclusivity, demonstrated by my ability to spark new friendships and build connections. Research shows strong social connections enhance academic performance and overall well-being. Additionally, my willingness to both delegate and follow leadership fosters efficient teamwork, which is crucial for successful clubs and projects. Finally, my commitment to service aligns with your college's focus on social responsibility, as evidenced by the (specific program offered by the college).

Just be sure to note that the examples in the box above are begging for details. The devil is in the details! Without specific details and examples for each of the claims they make, they are empty of meaning. If you spent 650 words beginning with any of these sentences and then showing how the various claims they make are true, then you're on your way to college essay gold.

Take, for example, the claim *"Additionally, my willingness to both delegate and follow leadership fosters efficient teamwork, which is crucial for successful clubs and projects."*

This is an empty sentence unless you show: where and when have you delegated leadership? When and where have you followed leadership? How were any of these crucial for the success of which club and which project?

2. Tone: The attitude of the storyteller in the story and mood created in the reader.

When we speak of tone, it is important to understand that tone inhabits the entire piece of writing—tone is everywhere in the story. In this sense, all elements of style contribute to the creation of tone.

Another way to understand tone is through the word persona. As the author of your story, you create a storyteller with a unique personality and worldview, and this persona exists only in the storytelling.

(You can think of this as a narrator, but the word persona better conveys the unique nature of this 650 word story you are telling, one that exists solely for the task of persuasion!)

The same event in a story can be told by completely different personas with completely different tones. Is your tone joyful or regretful? Inspirational or pessimistic? Humorous or melancholic?

Tone

Weak:

You should admit me to your college is because I have excelled in academics, given my best to sports, and maximized my involvement in extracurriculars. (lacks personality)

Humorous tone:

Basically, let's just cut to the chase: admit me already! My transcript is basically a trophy case, I hustle harder than a barista on finals week, and I'm pretty sure my extracurricular involvement qualifies me for a small-town mayor position.

Regretful tone:

Knowing what I've poured into academics, athletics, and extracurriculars, I truly believe [College Name] would be a perfect fit. Perhaps my application didn't fully capture that.

Modest Tone:

Given the current state of college admissions, with everyone else probably boasting similar achievements, admitting me to your school might be a long shot. But hey, I excelled in academics, gave my all to sports (well, most of the time), and stretched myself thin across extracurriculars. What more could you ask for in a slightly above-average applicant?

---

3. Imagery: The use of the five senses of sight, sound, touch, taste, and smell.

This is something you have definitely heard more than a few times in English class: Show don't tell! Or maybe you remember that your English teacher got all excited by "vivid description" in a novel but you were nodding off and couldn't care less what the fuss was about.

Imagery

Weak:

Dracula lay in a coffin aboard the ship Demeter wondering if the time was right to transform and attack the captain and his shipmates.

Strong:

The sodden earth clinging to the inner coffin tickled Dracula's pale nose, mocking his inaction while the rhythmic groaning of the Demeter provided a counterpoint to the frantic desires of his undead heart. A shaft of moonlight, weak and diluted by the grime of the hold, cast an eerie glow on the chipped wood of his resting place. His fangs ached as a primal urge to tear and rend coursed through him. He could almost taste the coppery tang of blood pumping through the veins of the unsuspecting captain and his mates.

---

4. The Devil is in the Details: Accomplished through the use of context, facts, and situational vocabulary.

If you describe an experience and want to make it yours and yours alone, you must avoid generalizations and instead invest time to record the specifics, the details that convince the reader that your experience is significant.

Example: You want to write about playing Lacrosse.

Context: You play Lacrosse for the varsity team.

Facts: The game transitions between a settled offense and fast breaks. On defense, players need to stay in their zones and check their opponents away from the goal

Situational vocabulary: cage, man-down, face-off, cradling, alley, dodge, boxing, lemons, all-outs.

The Devil is in the Details: Lacrosse

Weak:

I enjoyed playing varsity Lacrosse because it taught me the value of teamwork.

Strong:

The grind of varsity lacrosse wasn't just about ripping a perfect bounce shot or executing a flawless spin dodge. It was the camaraderie built during countless hours of ground ball drills, trust forged during tight man-down defenses, and exhilaration when a perfectly timed feed found an open teammate—all testaments to the power of teamwork that the sport instilled into me."

Example: You learned ballet.

Context: You learned ballet all through childhood and into middle school.

Facts: Ballet is a classical dance with formal moves that allows dancers to master complicated and demanding techniques to interpret music and let the human body tell a story with emotional power.

Situational vocabulary: plié, tendu, dégagé, sauté, petit jetée, barre, planks, assemblé, pointe, port de bras, détourné, phrasing, sissonne ouverte.

The Devil is in the Details: Ballet

Weak:

Through my years of ballet from kindergarten through middle school, I learned the value of sacrifice, perseverance, and discipline.

Strong:

After eight strenuous yet rewarding years of ballet, my body speaks tendus, pliés, and dégagés. Over countless hours spent at the barre building strength and refining positions, I've come to understand that there is no shortcut to excellence. Ballet challenges the body to overcome its limitations and the price is paid in sweat and tears, fatigue and soreness. It is only through unwavering discipline that I finally nailed a sissonne ouverte, and that moment of gravity-defying magic made all the sacrifices worthwhile.

---

5. Figurative Language: The use of figurative tools and devices to create both a depth of meaning and a pleasurable experience for the reader.

Why do we use simile and metaphor? Symbol and personification? Allusion and alliteration?

The short answer is that all these tools extend the range of meaning by invoking a network of associated possibilities. These tools invite the reader to contemplate the fact that life is a tapestry of connections in which the significance of any situation always contributes to our understanding of the larger picture of life.

Hidden in every particular instance of your life lurks a universal theme—and using the figurative tools of language broadens the scope of your story.

Simile

Weak:

When it came to protecting those that I had turned to my cause, I was fiercely protective.

Strong:

Like a hawk ready to swoop down on its prey, I was ever vigilant in protecting those I had turned to my cause.

Metaphor

Weak:

I surveyed the city of London, teeming with its millions going about their routines unmindful of the calamity about to strike them down.

Strong:

The inhabitants of the city of London are so many little cogs grinding in a doomsday clock, unmindful that the big hand is about to strike the hour of reckoning.

Symbol

Weak:

My adversaries relied on religion and superstition in their attempt to counter me, but it seems that this mindset of blind belief is human folly–countless others have relied on blind faith in their attempts to stop me from achieving the true conversion: human to vampire.

Symbol:

My adversaries might well have brandished a horseshoe instead of a crucifix for all the good it did them in their efforts to stop me from effectuating true conversion: human to vampire.

Personification

Weak:

The syringes were injected into each person's arm, drawing blood between them in long curving tubes.

Strong:

The tube slithered on the floor as syringes on each of its ends punctured the veins of each person's arm, and it began pulsing with fresh blood.

Allusion

Weak:

Darwin went to the Galapagos islands to study adaptation and natural selection of the species, and decided that humans have no natural predator; I beg to differ–I am at the apex of all food chains and yes, humans are prey.

Strong:

It falls on me to rectify an omission in the theory of evolution and author The Origin of the Vampire Species to inform humans that they too are prey and I alone hunt at the apex.

Alliteration

Weak:

Not all servants ascend to vampire state. My kiss is reserved for the worthy few whose spirit will never bow down and whose pride cannot be diminished.

Strong:

That raging Renfield could never understand that stalwart servitude is no guarantee of ascension, that my kiss was reserved for those whose spirit never kneels and whose pride defies debasement.

6. Diction: The use of the correct choice of word for maximum impact.

If it is the story of your journey in life so far in a mere 650 words, then every word in this story must be a strategic choice. Diction will help you establish the tone of your story—do you want to sound curious or knowledgeable? Are you poetic or logical? Is there a serious or a humorous person hidden behind the writing?

Another aspect of diction is the subtext: what do you want to convey about yourself in addition to the literal message? If you use precise academic jargon, your reader will assume you are research oriented; if, on the other hand, your choice of words leans on abstract concepts, you might be telling the reader that you are a Socrates in the making.

There is another aspect of diction that cannot be overstated: **do not use negative diction!** Words such "hate," "dislike," "resentment," "irritation," and "disgust" should have no place in the story you are choosing to tell. The overuse of such words will create a subtext of negativity around your persona—and how is that ever going to help you gain admission?

7. Syntax: The arrangement of words and phrases in a sentence as well as the type of possible sentences.

Whether or not you are a fan of the Star Wars saga, you must be acquainted with the legendary Jedi master Yoda and the quirky manner in which he speaks profound truths such as:

"Luminous beings are we."

"Always in motion is the future."

"A teacher Yoda is."

Yoda-speak inverts the conventional order of an English sentence which in its active voice follows the sequence Subject - Verb - object.

Subject (Doer of the action)	Verb (action-word)	Object (receiver of the action)
We	are	luminous beings.
Yoda	is	a teacher.
The future	is	always in motion.

Why does Yoda speak a large majority of his sentences in the Object-Verb-Subject form? Is it to show that he's not originally from earth? Or is it to show that English is not his first language? Or perhaps, it might be to paint his pronouncements with a philosophical brush: Deep thinker is Yoda! Wise is Yoda!

Yoda is not alone in playing with syntax; Shakespeare was mighty fond of it as well: "To be or not to be, that is the question" (*Hamlet*), "Hardly ever does she visit," (*Romeo and Juliet*), "His two chamberlains will I with wine convince" (*Macbeth*).

The point being you can choose to give any of your sentences a dramatic or even playful twist.

Moreover, as the author of the story of your journey so far, you should equip yourself with another syntax-related arsenal: types of sentences.

8. Types of Sentence/Rhythm: The use of a variety of sentence types creates rhythm in the story telling.

The complaint made against "bad" club music is that it is monotonous, that it is one repetitive beat (boom-boom-boom-boom (pause) boom-boom-boom-boom (pause and repeat). A repetitive beat with no variation bores the listener; likewise, repetitive sentence structure bores the reader.

Your story must have rhythm to keep the reader engaged, and there is no better way to ensure rhythm than by varying the type of sentences that you employ. Familiarize yourself with the types listed below and use them in a mindful manner so that you have an assortment that creates a pleasing rhythm.

Let us review the two types of clauses that go into sentence formation, independent clause and dependent clause:

An independent clause contains a subject (doer of the action), verb (the action), and object (receiver of the action), and is a complete thought.

> Example: independent clause
>
> *We are luminous beings.*
> *The future is always in motion.*

A dependent clause contains a subject (doer of the action), verb (the action) and an object (receiver of the action), but is an incomplete thought.

> Example: dependent clause
>
> *Although we are luminous beings.*
> *While the future is always in motion.*

A simple sentence has one independent clause. Note: this doesn't mean that the sentence has to be short since it can be lengthened by modifiers and complements.

> Example: simple sentence
>
> *We are luminous beings.*
> *We are luminous beings who traverse vast distances.*
> *We are luminous beings gifted with the foresight to make wise decisions at all times.*

A compound sentence has two independent clauses joined by a coordinating conjunction (for, and, nor, but, or, yet, so), a conjunctive adverb (however, therefore), or just a plain semicolon.

> Example: Compound sentence
>
> *We are luminous beings, and Yoda is our teacher.*
>
> *The future is always in motion, but luminous beings can stop the flow of time.*
>
> *Yoda is known as a great teacher; however, his claim to fame is the fact that he fought Palpatine.*

A **complex sentence** has an independent clause joined by a dependent clause using subordinating conjunction (after, although, as, as long as, because, before, despite, even if, even though, if, in order that, rather than, since, so that, though, unless, until, when, where, whereas, whether, and while).

> Example: complex sentence
>
> *Although we are luminous beings, Yoda is our teacher.*
>
> *While luminous beings can stop the flow of time, the future is always in motion.*
>
> *Even though Yoda's claim to fame is the fact that he fought Palpatine, he did not defeat him.*

A **periodic sentence** is a long sentence with many modifying phrases used to create suspense, drama, or surprise by withholding the independent clause to the very end of the sentence.

> Example: periodic sentence
>
> *Dust motes danced in the golden light filtering through the Senate chamber windows, tremors ran down Yoda's arm as he tightened his grip on his cane, his expression wearing a serene facade while his energy tapped into the Force, and his lightsaber began humming to life under his cloak, and just as the dark shadows began pulsing, he exclaimed, "Palpatine, Come for you I have!"*

A **cumulative sentence** reveals the independent clause at the beginning and then follows up with a series of subordinate clauses and phrases to enrich the main idea with a ton of supporting details.

> Example: cumulative sentence
>
> *Yoda taught Luke Skywalker the ways of the Force on swampy Dagobah, beneath a shroud of mist that clung to the gnarled trees like ghostly cloaks, his green skin wrinkled with centuries of wisdom, his voice a melodic rasp, pushing Luke Skywalker, a farm boy thrust into a galactic war, to control his impatience, to hone his skills until his movements became a blur, and to open himself entirely, not just with his mind but with every fiber of his being, to the flowing, ever-present Force that pulsed through the very lifeblood of the galaxy.*

A **balanced sentence** uses parallel structure and keeps equal weight in each part of the parallel element to emphasize the equal importance of each clause or phrase.

Example: balanced sentence

As Yoda fought Palpatine, lightsabers clashed in a blinding fury, energy sparkled with desperate desire, strikes landed at superhuman speed, and the Jedi watched with increasing awe.

A short sentence is a simple sentence usually of 3 to 5 words to create a dramatic effect in the midst of a paragraph with longer sentence structures.

Example: short sentence

As Yoda fought Palpatine, lightsabers clashed in a blinding fury, energy sparkled with desperate desire, strikes landed at superhuman speed, and the Jedi watched with increasing awe. The end was near.

The Rule of 3s: whenever you have a list, it is aesthetically pleasing to keep it limited to exactly 3 items, no more and no less. Two items is insufficient, four or more items is overkill. Whatever purpose the list serves, keep it limited to 3.

Tricolon is a nifty variation on the rule of 3s—a series of three parallel words, phrases, or clauses. Using tricolons gives a sense of enjoyment to the reader and also imparts a sense of completeness.

Example: Tricolon (Rule of 3s)

Be Sincere, be brief, be seated. (FDR)

Tell me and I forget. Teach me and I remember. Involve me and I learn. (Ben Franklin)

I require three things in a man. He must be handsome, ruthless, and stupid. (Dorothy Parker)

You are talking to a man who has laughed in the face of death, sneered at doom, and chuckled at catastrophe. (The Wizard of Oz)

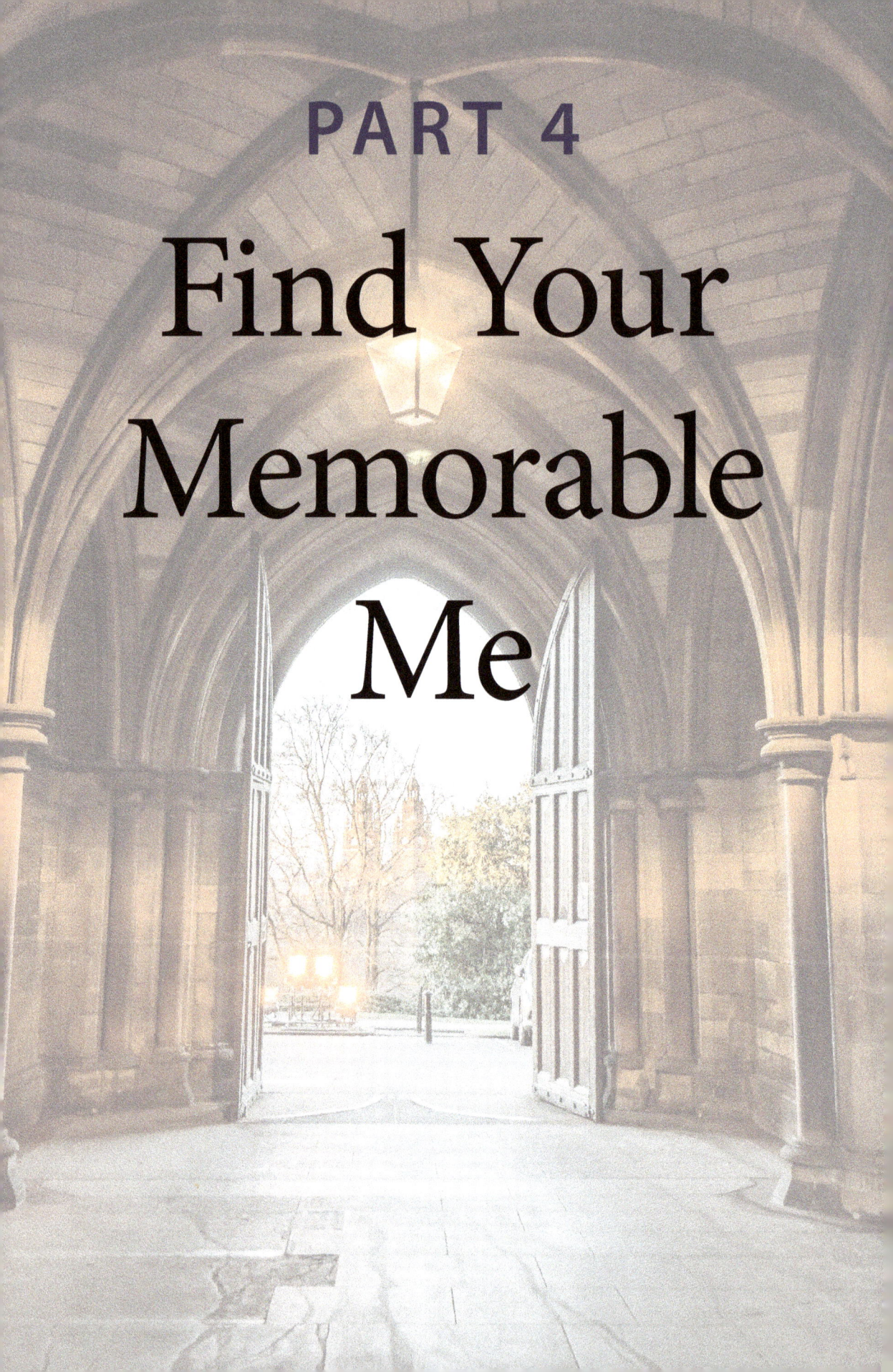

PART 4

Find Your Memorable Me

CHAPTER 10
Find Your Memorable Me

Dracula, while you have done an admirable job addressing the prompts with specifics and details that showcase the range of your experiences and interests, the truth is that most if not all the essays do not adequately serve the purpose of the exercise: write your way into gaining an offer for admission from the college of your choice.

Note: while there are 7 essay prompts on the Common Application, there is actually only one question being asked by all 7 prompts. Namely,

In more or less 650 words, what can you tell me (the admissions officer) that will excite me enough to offer you admission to my fine campus?

Or,

What can you say to convince me (the admissions officer) of the fact that you belong amongst the amazing college students on my amazing college campus?

Or,

What interests, experiences, and/or pursuits can you bring to my college that will enrich the campus experience and the lives of your fellow students?

 Pro Tip: Every sentence in The College Essay has to be about you and you only, not any of the millions of high schoolers applying with you. Contextualize everything you say through your own, heroic story.

In its essence, The College Essay is not really an essay at all! The "college essay" is a misnomer for what, in fact, is a narrative about your life. By narrative here, we mean a story: a story about your life. Yet, the story has the specific purpose of answering the questions posed above. In fact, the question being asked can be rephrased as the following prompt:

Tell us a memorable and authentic story of your journey so far that will differentiate you from all the other equally well-qualified candidates and convince us to select you for admission.

For this story of your life to work, it needs to have some vital components. The story about your life needs to:

- Show the major influences that shaped you into becoming who you are—the hero of your own journey.
- Show the major experiences you have chosen to pursue in life, the ones that shaped the kind of hero you're becoming.
- Show how your life so far has fostered interests for your future journey, interests whose pursuits will launch you into your hero's journey in college and beyond.

The word "journey" is of paramount importance. Your story needs to show that you have been on a journey of discoveries and experiences, and that you are excited to continue that journey of discovery and experience in college.

 Pro Tip: What do they NOT know about you yet? That's what The College Essay is all about. They have your entire application & portfolio—outside of that, what's your story.

So, how are you to write the story of "My Journey So Far"?

Well, the first thing you have to realize is that **you are the hero of your journey.**

If you are, indeed, the hero of the story "My Journey So Far," then you must think about:

What is my quest?

Why is it my quest?

What makes my quest unique?

How will college help my quest?

How will my quest help the world?

you are probably thinking—how am I supposed to answer all this in 650 words?!

To answer this question, let your mind go blank and think back to all the English classes in school, the ones you loved and the ones that put you to sleep, and answer the following question: what makes a story interesting, compelling, or memorable?

Themes. Remember those? **Universal themes!**

Believe it or not, all those years in English class were leading up to this very moment: the moment when you get to write a story about yourself with your themes and use that story to portray a memorable hero worthy of admission to the college of your choice.

Pro Tip: Colleges keep track of demonstrated interest: campus visits, informational sessions, phone calls, and even the number of "clicks" you have on their websites. Meet College reps & sign-in wherever you can!

And, you are in good hands. I have created a step-by-step workshop that will enable you to discover the major themes in your heroic journey so far, link those themes to specific experiences and moments of discovery, and **showcase a version of you that will be both memorable and authentic.** Trust the process, and you will end up with an essay that will stand out from the pile of college essays that admissions committees have to read.

So, let us begin to workshop how to write this "Story of My Journey So Far"!

Everyone is familiar with the adage: stories are meant to show not tell.

 Pro Tip: What makes you and your story memorable does not include usage of electronic devices or computers, and definitely not playing video games and scrolling through Tik-Toks.

But what do you show about yourself? And, how do you show yourself to be the hero of your journey without thumping your chest or yawping your name from the rooftops?

Relax! It is only a Five Step process. Work your way through the worksheets designed to get you from zero to hero. The best part is that you will discover who you are—what makes you tick and what makes you unique.

Step 1: Getting To Know Myself

What could be more fun than that? You will work your way through a bunch of questions about who you are—and none of these questions can be dismissed with an easy "yes" or "no" answer. For example: "What is your idea of happiness?"

Step 2: Discovering My Vital Themes

What are the thematic topics that excite you, motivate you, drive you? Are you all about tolerance or about innovation? Do you espouse open-mindedness or champion advocacy? Take a quick dive and find out the vital qualities—the themes that drive who you are, the qualities that make you tick.

 Pro Tip: Almost every successful college essay has the following themes embedded in its story: Caring & Collaboration, Passion & Perseverance. Keep these qualities in mind when you tell your story.

Step 3: My Vital Themes In Action

Talk is cheap. Telling me what makes you tick is boring: you are falling asleep as you write and I'm falling asleep as I read. **SHOW!** Show me specific moments in your life: jot down an **action/experience/encounter** that shows how whatever vital theme you picked became central to your life.

Step 4: Launch "My Journey So Far"

Take any one of the items you did in Step 3 and write out a short story that shows how the item became important in your life. You are almost there. If it doesn't work with one of your entries, try writing a story for another one of those entries. Keep your vital themes handy as you write.

> **Did You Know:** Setbacks in life make for great college essay stories as long as your focus is on the process of overcoming a negative situation (how did this journey make you the resilient young adult I would want on my college campus?)

Step 5: Complete Draft of "My Journey So Far"

Follow the guidelines and make sure the story embeds the Five Cardinal Components. And, hey presto, you are done! Congratulations!

Step 1: Getting to Know Myself

Getting to know yourself. Easier than it sounds.

The first step in discovering your authentic and memorable me is to spend some time with these open-ended questions. Your well thought out answers will launch you into a discovery of experiences and beliefs that are unique to you and no one else.

Yes, you are unique. Yes, you are an original. Yes, you are special. But how much do you know about what makes you tick?

It is time to find out!

 Pro Tip: In the late 1800s and way before the days of Snapchat and Discord, friends used to have friends answer these questions in a confession album. Date night, anyone?

Answer the questions below. Have fun with them. Be truthful. Be soul-searching. Be creative. Find out what makes you different from everyone around you.

These questions will help you get started on the journey of self-discovery.

Write a few sentences for each—the more you give, the more you'll get.

I have attached Count Dracula's answers to the list of questions below.

1. What is your current state of mind?

Frustration. That's being me right now. Frustration at the fact that I don't know how to go about writing The College Essay that will razzle and dazzle my readers into giving me admissions. I'm the most amazing being on earth—how do I convey that? Apparently, just telling everyone I'm Count Dracula worked against me. I don't know what they want. So yes, I'm frustrated.

2. What is your idea of happiness?

Commingling. Commingling of blood, commingling of spirit, commingling of being. Commingling is the reason I exist and the reason I convert my prey into the likeness of my being. Not my prey (I see you and your optics, Dr. Sood) but my novitiates. People mistakenly believe that they are meant to exist as individual islands forever distanced from each other in the ocean of being and becoming, but mine is the continent that drifts to assimilate all into a state of commingled existence. Commingling is my idea of happiness.

3. Who makes you laugh more than anyone?

Laugh? Who has time to laugh? (I guess I'll come back to this). Later: it is awkward writing this, but my life isn't predicated on humor. That is to say, I've done a lot of thinking, and it turns out that no one really makes me laugh. Why? I laugh at the helplessness of those who try to resist my conversion, but there is no mirth in my smile, only mockery. But, making me laugh? My DNA isn't wound up for laughter. Strange…I've never really thought about it—what does genuine laughter feel like?

4. What do you consider your greatest achievement?

Easy. The gift of immortality. Elevating weak and fallible mortals into the vampire state of being.

5. Best gift you ever received?

Received? I don't need gifts. I take what I want. (I guess I'll come back to this) Later: My novitiates, converts, minions—call them what you want—will offer me tokens of their servitude at all times. Sometimes, they offer their richly fed veins for me to tap, sometimes they bring me creatures big and small. Yet, those aren't gifts properly speaking. Those are expected to be given and given out of a sense of obeisance to me. Gifts, like laughter, is something I don't get.

6. What is your most treasured possession?

The ability to transform. It is the activity that makes me feel most like myself is transformation. It's that moment when I am in-between states of being, when I am neither human, nor bat, nor wolf, nor dust. At that moment, I am a universe of possibility and feel oneness with all that exists and will ever exist. I would not lose this ability for the world.

 Pro Tip: Probably the best decision you will ever make when choosing which college to attend is to prioritize graduating with as little debt as possible.

7. Which person past or present do you most admire?

I've never really thought about this. I don't know. Later: There is a woman who comes to mind, one whose child had been consumed by my three mistresses. She came wailing and imploring, angry and inconsolable, screaming and begging for the return of her child and realizing all along that it was too late. Not knowing how long she would raise that painful din, I summoned the wolves to come take care of her. Yet, just as they were about to devour her, that bereft mother grew silent and turned to face them. She was defiant in her last moments and silent despite the physical suffering of the wolvish jaws tearing her to shreds. I secretly admire this woman. In her abject sorrow and weakness, she found inner power.

8. Your favorite occupation when you are not working?

Watching sunsets. I have never felt calmer and safer than in those moments of watching the multihued glory of the setting sun. As it sinks over the horizon and turns the sky into a spectacle of orange and red hues, the sun reaffirms the natural order of things and the awakening of my vampire powers. It is a simple reaffirmation that everything is right with the world, that day will become night just as night will become day, and that my true self will awaken to prowl the world and shape it in my way.

9. If you could change one thing about yourself, what would it be??

I would get rid of my deadly allergies. It was by lucky accident that I even discovered there existed substances such as allergens, and that I was especially susceptible to those in the crucifix and the communal wafers. During the course of Lucy's blood transfusions, I began to realize the possibilities of modern science. I became a believer. It put me on the path to discovering the cause of my allergic reaction to crucifixes and the like, isolating the allergens, and helping invent the epipen.

10. What do you most value in your friends?

Open Mindedness. I am grateful for those that are receptive to the gift of immortality. A mutual commingling is always so much more satisfying than a forced one. I am grateful that there are always going to be Lucy Westenras in my life, those who are open minded but also reciprocate my ardor with uninhibited passion.

11. If not yourself, who would you be?

Believe it or not, I would be my nemesis, Dr. Van Helsing. I will never forget the image of the blood transfusion Van Helsing administered to Lucy. It was the first time that I had seen such paraphernalia—tourniquets, syringes, and tubes—as Dr. Van Helsing linked Arthur with Lucy to transfer his blood into the body whose blood I had feasted on the previous night. I was in disbelief—they were replicating with science and instruments what for centuries I had conducted with biology and fangs! The image of Arthur reclining on his armchair as his blood pumped into the veins of Lucy—fattening her up for my next feed—is one I'll never forget because it marked the moment when I realized the rapid rise of scientific inquiry and achievement by mortals and gave me an impetus to start delving more deeply into the various domains of 20th-century science.

12. If you had a clone, what would you have it do?

If I had a clone I would delegate him to be the exclusive caretaker of my finances, accounts, and operational logistics around the globe. Maintaining my global estate is time consuming. Although I have several corporations with hundreds of employees dedicated to the task of keeping Dracula Inc. profitable, I waste so much time at board meetings to ensure accountability and productivity. My clone wouldn't like it, but I would make him the global in-command for all the corporate work—and that would free me up to do what I love doing best.

13. What is your pet peeve?

This college essay?! But seriously…what really irks me is a millennia-long conundrum I still have to solve: branding. My name and image is inextricably linked with evil. Try as I might, I am unable to rebrand myself away from the image of a bloodthirsty and evil vampire. If I say that I am driven by love not hate, by a desire to give and not take, and by a will for inclusion and not subjugation then I am faced with utter disbelief. I am not the enemy but the savior— but how do I go about changing my image, rebranding my legacy? It's a question that continues to perplex me.

14. When and where are you happiest?

I am happiest when I am lost in acquiring knowledge or gaining expertise. It could be being immersed in a book, in a sparring session at the dojo, or in an experiment at the genetics lab— but these and a thousand more activities in which I lose track of time and need for rest are when I feel happiest.

15. What talent would you most like to have?

Easy. The talent I would most like to have is the one that I short-circuited myself from having when I battled and defeated Feurix: the power to access my Dracula qualities throughout the day. The power to not have to slumber in dirt in a coffin in order to replenish my state of being. Feurix was canny and deceptive, having led me to believe that I could decipher the right spells from his book of secret incantations. But I've spent centuries going over the contents and had no success. So yes, the talent I would like to have is the ability to function as me during broad daylight.

16. What is your greatest extravagance?

Lifestyle and Luxury. I have had millennia to access riches and treasure. I have shamelessly expanded my empire of wealth, estate, and holdings. Long live shell corporations!

17. What is the trait you most deplore in yourself?

I broached on this incident in one of my college essay drafts—my underestimation of the Van Helsing gang. Had I not taken them so lightly, I would surely have commingled with Mina Harker till the end of nights. She was the one and she wanted me as much as I wanted her, and my overconfidence made me rash and arrogant. This led to a series of missteps that allowed the emboldened Van Helsing gang to defeat me.

18. Your idea of misery?

Losing my powers of seduction. What good would life be without the power of being able to peel away resistance infinitesimal layer by infinitesimal layer, at being able to tap into the secret, forbidden, and even unknown desires of my prey, and at being able to caress and whisper visions of fulfillment into their souls—which soon enough are conceded to my dominion.

19. What is your greatest fear?

Fear is of the unknown and very little is unknown to me. People fear the vampire in the dark but what does the vampire Dracula fear? Being apprehended in the light, perhaps. But to avoid this situation, I have always designed escape routes and have never been caught. Take the incident at Borgo Pass, for instance. When Harker slit my throat with his Nepali Kukri knife and Quincy plunged his American Bowie knife into my heart, Were they not a fraction of second too late? Had not the Szgany in my employ delayed them in the knife fight just long enough for the sun to sink behind the mountain pass? Did they not understand the triumph they saw in my eyes right before they assaulted my body?

20. What can you do better?

Smile. I can smile better. As everyone knows, I don't have the most photogenic teeth. And other than protruding canines, my smile is seen as a menace by most. I have yet to discover the right intent for a smile—never have I tried a smile but that I have felt sudden recoil from my audience. I love to do it anyway, perhaps it is perverse of me. But trust me, I smile and smile, and whether they like it or not, know that I also chuckle on the inside.

21. Who broke your heart?

Figuratively, no one. But almost literally, Mina Harker. How often have I wished for a time machine to take me back to Mina Harker's London and hand over an entire supply of epipens to my Victorian self at Dr. Seward's Sanatorium. We were in throes of vampiric ecstasy with Mina at my chest, consuming the blood pumping from the fervent chambers of my heart when, armed with their crucifixes and beads and wafers, that loathsome crew interrupted our love making. Instead of sanguis interruptus, Mina and I would have climaxed our union and conversion in plain sight of the interfering interlopers!

22. What is the trait you most deplore in others?

That's easy. Dependency. I would like to get rid of the responsibility of having to chaperone my hordes, reigning in their bloodlust. Contrary to movies that have distorted the truth, only my bite elevates humans into the vampire state of being. The hordes I have spawned, however, only suck on human blood for survival. And they tend to be indiscriminate in terms of target, time, and place when it comes to satisfying their craving. As a result, I'm always summoned to put out their fires. Though they vow subservience to me, they undermine my larger goal of gaining worldwide acceptance for vampire conversion.

23. What is your greatest regret?

My greatest regret is underestimating human ingenuity and inventiveness. Look at where society was and where it is today. Centuries ago, I considered myself superior in all facets of being; today, I am reconciled with the fact that I am superior in longevity, strength, and transformability but not in intellect, resolve, and creativity. I have to remain ever vigilant to not make the mistake of discounting human capabilities.

24. What do you tolerate the least?

Not being seen for who I am and my true potential. At the root of the matter, this is why I had to challenge Feurix in a battle to the death. It was by far the hardest decision I've ever made. I knew that my success would mean his death, and his death would mean the loss of access to the trove of magical knowledge I desperately wanted. However, I believed that Feurix was toying with me, belittling me at every turn, delaying and denying me access to what he knew. Could he not see that I was an insatiable mind in an indefatigable body, absorbing all he had to offer in a fraction of an instant compared to all his other disciples?

25. What is your favorite painting?

Love and Pain by Edvard Munch. It is a fantasy, showing a red haired woman giving the vampire's kiss on the back of the neck of a submissive male hunched below her embrace. It captures my vision of empowerment for all my converted brides. May they forever dominate the frailty of humanity!

26. Three words that describe you?

Judicious. Perspicacious. Passionate.

27. Three words that others use to describe you?

Powerful. Cunning. Hypnotic.

28. What are you listening to?

The entire album from the Queen of the Damned soundtrack.

29. On what occasion do you lie?

All is fair in love and war and all war is deception. This dictum has never been truer for style love making. I have been forever attacked by those who wish to deny humanity the evolution I offer. And yet, I am always triumphant because there is no greater practitioner of the art of deception than yours truly. Who else taught Sun Tzu: when able to attack, seem unable; when using force, appear inactive; when nearing the enemy, appear to be retreating; when far away, appear to be nearing. Lies are deception and means to an end.

 Pro Tip: Speak from a place of truth and lived experience. Lying is easy, lying well is next to impossible. People who lie well are fiction writers by profession. Make sure that your college essay conveys true experiences about the journey of your life so far!

30. What do you consider the most overrated virtue?

Holiness is the most overrated virtue. It allows the sanctimonious to preach against my conversion all the while enabling their own corruption. Holiness is virtue become institution, one designed to subjugate the masses for its own avarice.

Step 2: Discovering My Vital Themes

You are the hero of the story of your life, "My Journey So Far." Cue in your favorite English class here: "every story has themes that are vital to its message."

What are the thematic topics that excite you, motivate you, drive you?

What have you come to believe strongly in? What is of fundamental importance to the hero that you are becoming in your "Journey So Far"?

1. Circle as many Vital Themes below that resonate with you.

Abundance	Diversity	Learning	Resourcefulness
Acceptance	Empathy	Love	Responsibility
Achievement	Encouragement	Loyalty	Responsiveness
Adaptability	Enthusiasm	Making a difference	Security
Advancement	Ethics	Mindfulness	Self-Control
Adventure	Excellence	Motivation	Selflessness
Advocacy	Expressiveness	Optimism	Simplicity
Ambition	Fairness	Open-mindedness	Stability
Appreciation	Family	Originality	Success
Autonomy	Fashion	Performance	Teamwork
Balance	Friendship	Personal development	Thoughtfulness
Being the Best	Flexibility	Proactive	Traditionalism
Benevolence	Freedom	Professionalism	Trustworthiness
Boldness	Fun	Quality	Understanding
Brilliance	Generosity	Recognition	Uniqueness
Calmness	Gratitude	Risk-taking	Usefulness
Caring	Grace	Safety	Versatility
Challenge	Growth	Service	Vision
Charity	Harmony	Spirituality	Warmth
Cheerfulness	Happiness	Stability	Wealth
Cleverness	Health	Perfection	Well-Being
Community	Humility	Peace	Wisdom
Commitment	Humor	Playfulness	Zeal
Compassion	Inclusiveness	Popularity	(add your own below)
Cooperation	Interdependence	Power	
Collaboration	Individuality	Preparedness	
Consistency	Innovation	Proactivity	
Contribution	Inquiry	Professionalism	
Creativity	Inspiration	Punctuality	
Curiosity	Intelligence	Recognition	
Daring	Intuition	Relationships	
Decisiveness	Joy	Reliability	
Dedication	Kindness	Resilience	
Dependability	Knowledge		
	Leadership		

2. Copy down all the Vital Themes you circled:

Adaptability, advancement, challenge, decisiveness, growth, intelligence, knowledge, leadership, learning, originality, power, preparedness, responsibility, uniqueness

3. Narrow it down to your top 5 Vital Themes:

CHALLENGE	LEARNING	MASTERY	PREPAREDNESS	UNIQUENESS

4. Pick your top three Vital Themes and copy them down in the box below:

My Vital Themes

UNIQUENESS	PREPAREDNESS	LEARNING

5. Crosscheck: Take your Vital Themes and cross-reference them with your responses in the "Getting to Know Myself" worksheet.

Are the Vital Themes reflected in the responses from worksheet #1?

Yes	No
Congratulations! You have your Vital Themes.	Go back to Step 1 above (and be truthful)

You can now begin crafting the story of "My Journey So Far"!

Step 3: My Vital Themes in Action

From the My Vital Themes exercise you did on the worksheet, enter the top three to five in the first column.

Then, in the second column, jot down an **action/experience/encounter** that shows how the theme is vital to your life. It could be something in the past, something in the present, or even something you foresee in the future.

Finally, in the third column, anchor the action onto an object/person that is key to the experience.

Vital Themes Ranked in order of importance	What is an action that shows how my theme is vital in my life?	What is an object/person that is memorable in that action?
1. PREPAREDNESS	Failed to convert Mina; fell prey to the allergens in the wafers etc. (essay #2)	Wafer, crucifix; epipen: the symbols of my weakness for centuries, but now combated by the tools of modern science such as the epipen.
2. UNIQUENESS	Looking into the mirror for the first time and seeing no reflection of myself. (essay#3)	Handheld mirror with split-leaf palmette design inlaid with gold; looking at xy and xxy chromosomes under the microscope and realizing I am xxy.
3. LEARNING	Seeing the blood-transfusion for the first time in Lucy's case opened my eyes to the possibilities of science in blood related matters (essay #4)	Blundell's blood transfusion apparatus that Dr. Van Helsing used to try to "save" Lucy.
4. CHALLENGE	Faced with an adversary who could actually defeat me, I challenged him to a duel unsure of whether I could win but sure that I needed to overcome him. (essay #5)	I remember raising a cairn of stones over the tumulus for Feurix. As I made a pile of stones, it began to thunder and rain, but I was not riding the dragon to make it so.
5. MASTERY	Desire and experience with a variety of crafts through the ages. (essay #6)	Double-grieved parmularius; Ashoka's steel alloy pillar, the granite stone at Badaling, Great Wall of China.

Step 4: Launch "My Journey So Far"

Now, take one item from your box in Step 3 and write out the short story behind it: why is it so vital to who you are? What happened to make it vital? Who was involved? Where and when did the story take place? What insight did you gain?

Tip #1: Show! This means using vivid description, engaging the five senses: touch, taste, sight, sound, and smell.

Tip #2: Look at the work you did in choosing the worksheets My Vital Themes and Vital Themes in Action. Use these Vital Themes and Vital Actions in telling your story.

Tip #3: Don't worry about the length/word count of your story (we will deal with that later!).

Tip #4: Give your story a title. But, do this only AFTER you have written out your story.

Dos and Don'ts for The College Essay

Do understand the question being asked of every essay regardless of the prompt: How will my college campus be enriched by the presence of this student?

Do show not tell how you are a great young adult ready for college and campus life

Do be the hero of the story of your journey in life so far

Do show what really matters: passion and perseverance

Do show what really matters: overcoming of obstacles and setbacks

Do show what really matters: caring & collaboration

Do be a memorable you and not a stereotype of you and everyone else

Do make your reader feel inspiration: the world would be a better place if it were populated with more people like you!

Don't use negative diction

Don't use word choice you are not familiar with

Don't use cliches

Don't state the obvious

Don't explain the obvious

Don't get lost in telling (and not showing)

Don't get lost in ruminations & philosophizing

Special Item: Blundell's apparatus for Blood Transfusion

Title: An Impeller and a Gravitator

Story:

I hovered unnoticed outside Lucy Westenra's window. Inside, two men I knew helped an unfamiliar third unpack equally unfamiliar instruments from a wooden case. They were variously brass and silver colored: a funnel, a couple of thin, curved and tapering pipes, a rod, and a formidable looking syringe. There was a flurry of activity, The stranger directed Dr. Seward, the head of the lunatic asylum, and Holmwood, Lucy's fiance, to assemble the pieces into a novel contraption. My curiosity turned to amazement as they inserted the tapering end of one silver pipe into a vein in Lucy's arm; the other into a similar vein in Holmwood's arm. What infernal device was this? What were they doing to my poor, beloved Lucy? Judging by her gaunt face, sunken eyes, and lifeless cheeks, she was but a slumber or two away from crossing over to the undead state of being and becoming one of my forever brides.

And yet, just as I was about to crash through the window and effect a gallant rescue, I noticed something miraculous—her pallor became suffused with a rosy flush and soon enough, life and color had returned to her face. The transformation was uncanny. There was only one explanation—these gentlemen had re-blooded my Lucy. The apparatus had managed some sort of transfusion of blood.

Through the ages, I had perfected the art of painlessly draining blood, but these gentlemen had engineered the reverse with the ingenious use of what turned out to be a lancet, a history, an impeller and a gravitator.

Step 5: Draft of "My Journey So Far"

Great news; in the previous worksheet, you already launched your story of your journey so far. This means that you already have a great hook and something original because it tells us what makes you the hero of your own life, a hero with a compelling story to share.

Now, your task is to complete the draft. Cut and paste your launch story. Then, transition from your launch story into any of the cardinal components listed below to complete your draft.

1. What you have experienced in life (impactful moments chosen for you by others like parents or caregivers)

2. What you have done in life (choices you made for yourself; the quests big and small you began to pursue because you wanted to)

3. Who you are today (show the caliber of your heroic personality with details of key academic & extracurricular pursuits)

4. What you want to do in the future (what are your heroic quests?)

5. Who you will become tomorrow (need not be explicit; steps 1-4 convey this)

Title of your story:

(story of "Mapping my Memorable Me" ~650 words)

I hovered unnoticed outside Lucy Westenra's window. Inside, two men helped an unfamiliar third unpack unfamiliar instruments from a wooden case. They were variously brass and silver colored: a funnel, a couple of thin, curved and tapering pipes, a rod, and a formidable looking syringe. There was a flurry of activity, The stranger directed Dr. Seward, the head of the lunatic asylum, and Holmwood, Lucy's fiance, to assemble the pieces into a novel contraption. My curiosity turned to amazement as they inserted the tapering end of one silver pipe into a vein in Lucy's arm; the other into a similar vein in Holmwood's arm. What infernal device was this? What were they doing to my poor, beloved Lucy? Judging by her gaunt face, sunken eyes and lifeless cheeks, she was but a slumber or two away from crossing over to the undead state of being and becoming my forever bride.

And yet, just as I was about to crash through the window and effect a gallant rescue, I noticed something miraculous—her pallor became suffused with a rosy flush and soon enough, life and color had returned to her face. The transformation was uncanny. There was only one explanation—these gentlemen had re-blooded my Lucy. The apparatus had managed some sort of transfusion of blood.

Through the ages, I had perfected the art of painlessly draining blood, but these gentlemen had engineered the reverse using Blundell's innovative apparatus.

From this moment forward, I became passionate about science—its experiments, its possibilities, its discoveries.

I applied to become a laboratory assistant in the Department of Pathological Anatomy at the University of Vienna. Working under Karl Landsteiner, I assisted in research in the field of morbid physiology and pathological anatomy. Aiding and observing the work of a group of tireless scientific pioneers, I felt exhilarated as they discovered new facts about immunological factors in syphilis, paroxysmal haemoglobinuria, and poliomyelitis. But my greatest joy was being present when Prof. Landsteiner's meticulous and systematic investigations into blood transfusions resulted in his classifying blood types as A, B AB, and O. It was in Vienna, too, that Landsteiner's lab launched the investigation into bleeding in the newborn; and although the discovery of Rh-factors in blood was documented by him in New York a couple of decades later, I kept close correspondence and felt equally elated as part of his team at the Rockefeller Institute for Medical Research.

While I am still fascinated by research into the chemistry of antigens, antibodies, and other immunological occurrences in human blood, the proliferation of scientific knowledge in genetics has whetted my appetite in many other directions. I would love to study the relevance of Mendelian inheritance in quantitative genetics, the gain of function in dominant negative alleles, as well as the genetic variance in response to environmental factors through haplotype mapping.

Even more exciting are the possibilities created by the overlap of once distinct scientific fields. Does genetic research fall under the domain of biology, chemistry, biochemistry, biophysics, data analytics, combinatorics, or even algorithms & programming?

I am excited to enroll in your college and gain exposure by taking courses in various departments. I would love to converse with professors about their research and would cherish the opportunity to participate in as many research teams as possible. I am equally looking forward to socializing on campus with similarly motivated peers.

My quest for knowledge is fueled by the desire to know more about not only what makes us different but also what makes us the same. In genetic terms, we are all 99.5% identical. That 0.5% difference, however, is what populates the world with a panorama of diversity and a kaleidoscope of difference. In learning about us, I will also learn about me. And the more I know about where I come from, the better I will be able to map out the journey of where I must go.

(world count: 650)

CHAPTER 11
What About AI and GPTs?

L et us consider the 3rd entry from Dracula's worksheet "Step 3: My Vital Themes in Action."

Chat Gpt in Action

Vital Theme: LEARNING, also: mastery, challenge

Action that shows how theme is vital in Dracula's life: Seeing the blood transfusion in Lucy Westenra's case opened up Dracula's eyes to the possibilities of science in blood related matters

What object/person is memorable in that action: Blundell's blood transfusion apparatus that Dr. Van Helsing used to try to save Lucy

So, let us shape the above data into A PROMPT for Chat Gpt:

Hey Chat Gpt: Write a college essay of 650 words from the viewpoint of Count Dracula where he discusses how surreptitiously witnessing the blood transfusion Dr. Van Helsing conducted in order to try to save Lucy Westenra's life opened up his eyes to the possibilities of science, especially because he's seeing Blundell's blood transfusion apparatus for the first time. Please embed the themes of learning, mastery, and challenge.

Chat Gpt's Essay:

An Elixir of Enlightenment: Dracula's Encounter with Science by Chatgpt

In the centuries I have roamed the shadowy realms of the night, my encounters with science have been fleeting and superficial. As Count Dracula, the immortal embodiment of darkness, I considered myself above the realm of mortal inventions. Yet, a clandestine encounter with Dr. Van Helsing's blood transfusion attempt to save Lucy Westenra's life unveiled the astonishing possibilities of science, sparking in me a thirst for learning, mastery, and facing the challenges that lay ahead.

The sight of Dr. Van Helsing's blood transfusion apparatus, particularly Blundell's invention, was unlike anything I had ever seen. This masterpiece of human ingenuity fascinated me, and I found myself surreptitiously drawn to observe the procedure. It was a moment of revelation, witnessing the interplay between medicine and mechanics, and the seamless integration of science into the fabric of human life.

Learning has always been an intrinsic part of my existence. Through the ages, I have amassed a vast reservoir of knowledge from ancient texts and arcane sources. However, the world of science, a domain of mortals, had remained elusive to me until that fateful night. Witnessing the blood transfusion, I realized that knowledge was not limited to the realms of the supernatural. Mortals, too, possessed the power to uncover the mysteries of life and wield that knowledge to heal and save lives.

Dr. Van Helsing's mastery over this medical procedure was awe-inspiring. As I watched him navigate the complexities of Blundell's apparatus with precision, I recognized the significance of mastering one's craft. Whether it be the art of manipulation, as I had honed to exert my influence over others, or the scientific brilliance displayed before me, mastery was an aspiration that transcended time and status.

For the first time, I felt an inclination to understand the intricacies of science. The pursuit of knowledge was no longer confined to my quest for power and immortality; it was an endeavor to comprehend the world that existed beyond the scope of darkness. I craved to understand the principles governing blood circulation and the mechanics of Blundell's apparatus. In this pursuit of understanding, I faced the challenge of bridging the gap between the supernatural and the natural, and embracing the complexity of human physiology.

Challenges had always been a part of my existence. The thrill of overcoming adversaries had fueled my existence for centuries. However, the challenge I now faced was different—it was an internal one. I had to conquer my reservations about embracing science as a source of empowerment rather than a threat to my dominion.

As I delved into the world of science, I came across the works of medical pioneers like William Harvey and their discoveries on the circulation of blood. Their findings complemented the knowledge I had gathered from my ancient sources, presenting a holistic understanding of life. I recognized that my pursuit of knowledge and mastery was not limited to a single realm but was an amalgamation of the supernatural and the scientific.

The blood transfusion experiment on Lucy Westenra offered me a profound insight into the interconnectedness of all beings. It reinforced the idea that humans were not mere prey but intricate creatures, each with a unique tapestry of life coursing through their veins. My understanding of life and death expanded, and I found myself pondering the implications of science on my own immortal existence.

The encounter with Dr. Van Helsing's experiment brought forth an unexpected harmony between the realms of darkness and the light of science. It demonstrated that the boundaries between the supernatural and the natural were not as impenetrable as I had assumed. Embracing science did not diminish my powers; instead, it enriched my understanding of the world and the beings I sought to coexist with.

In conclusion, the surreptitious witnessing of Dr. Van Helsing's blood transfusion endeavor marked a pivotal moment in my existence as Count Dracula. The themes of learning, mastery, and challenge were intricately woven into this transformative experience. I discovered that knowledge and mastery were not restricted to the supernatural realm, but a shared pursuit of all beings, mortal or immortal. My thirst for learning now encompassed the wonders of science, bridging the gap between the ages past and the possibilities of the future.

As I continued my journey through the annals of time, I carried with me the elixir of enlightenment that Dr. Van Helsing's experiment had bestowed upon me. The pursuit of knowledge, the mastery of one's craft, and the embrace of challenges would forever be etched in my immortal consciousness. As Count Dracula, I now stood at the precipice of a new era—a realm where the supernatural and the scientific coexisted in harmony, a testament to the enduring power of learning and the allure of mastering the mysteries of life itself. (Word Count 789)

This is a well written essay. It reads well and has some merits but also very significant flaws.

Merits:

Variety of sentence structure: Chat Gpt varies length and type of sentences to create a pleasing rhythm. Consider a sampling:

- **Compound sentence:** "My understanding of life and death expanded, and I found myself pondering the implications of science on my own immortal existence."
- **Complex sentence:** "As I continued my journey through the annals of time, I carried with me the elixir of enlightenment that Dr. Van Helsing's experiment had bestowed upon me."
- **Appositive:** As Count Dracula, the immortal embodiment of darkness, I considered myself above the realm of mortal inventions.
- **Em-dash:** However, the challenge I now faced was different—it was an internal one.
- **Verb -ing modifying clause:** Yet, a clandestine encounter with Dr. Van Helsing's blood transfusion attempt to save Lucy Westenra's life unveiled the astonishing possibilities of science, sparking in me a thirst for learning, mastery, and facing the challenges that lay ahead.

Appropriate vocabulary: the word choice or diction suits the message being conveyed. The words are employed in their correct connotations and fit seamlessly with the message being conveyed. Reading this, we feel that the writer is using words they are familiar with and not reaching for thesaurus in order to impress.

- Clandestine
- Ingenuity
- Revelation
- Integration
- Surreptitiously
- Arcane
- Elusive
- Revelation
- Intrinsic
- Transcended
- Intricacies
- Dominion

Figurative Language: metaphors, similes, imagery and the like are always welcome in fluid prose as they add a depth to the message by highlighting comparison & contrast, anchoring abstraction in concrete details.

- Elixir of Enlightenment
- Thirst for learning
- Fabric of human life
- Vast reservoir of knowledge
- Bridging the gap
- Embracing the complexity
- The thrill...fueled my existence
- Tapestry of life
- Precipice of a new era

Well and good. But as I pointed out to my bloodthirsty client the Count, pyrotechnics alone do not a college essay make! There are several shortcomings in this Chat Gpt essay:

Shortcomings:

Overkill of figurative language: The metaphors are overdone. Way too many! While such language is edifying as it breaks the monotony of informational and detailed language, it cannot be a substitute for information based on the first hand experience of the college applicant.

The Chat Gpt essay layers metaphor on metaphor—and while it makes the language flowery it will not fool any admissions officer into believing that they are reading important details that shaped the intellectual journey of the applicant.

Lack of details/specifics: As the saying goes, the devil (of any task) is in the details. The details provided in the Chat Gpt essay remain at the level of generalities. There are many missed opportunities where specifics could have been provided and would have gone a long way into legitimizing the validity of the experience and its impact on shaping the applicant's academic interests. For example:

- "I came across the works of medical pioneers like William Harvey and their discoveries on the circulation of blood."

  What are the details of this journey (how exactly did you "come across") and, more importantly, what are some of the "discoveries on the circulation of blood"? In fact, the reader would expect these specifics to also be discussed in light of Dracula's extensive first hand knowledge with the circulation of blood.

- "Their findings complemented the knowledge I had gathered from my ancient sources, presenting a holistic understanding of life."

  Again, what are the ancient sources? What specific findings complemented what aspects of knowledge from Dracula's ancient sources? Not providing such details is a big miss in terms of effective college essay writing.

- "My understanding of life and death expanded, and I found myself pondering the implications of science on my own immortal existence."

  Sounds good. But a careful reader would realize right away that this is a statement in generality not specificity. The statement is begging Chat Gpt to share at least one way in which Dracula's understanding of life and death "expanded." Likewise, we would love to know what were some of the "implications of science" of Dracula's immortal existence!

Too much telling, not enough showing: This is a direct corollary of a lack of specifics/ details. You can tell me you had a life changing revelation but **you have to show:** what is that revelation? What are the circumstances surrounding that revelation? As the saying goes, talk is cheap. Or indeed, you can talk the talk, but you have got to show how you walk the walk. For example:

- "The sight of Dr. Van Helsing's blood transfusion apparatus, particularly Blundell's invention, was unlike anything I had ever seen. This masterpiece of human ingenuity..."

  How about showing us the apparatus, how Van Helsing works it, what makes it a masterpiece?

- "a clandestine encounter with Dr. Van Helsing's blood transfusion attempt to save Lucy Westenra's life..."

  Where is the story of this clandestine encounter? Where did it take place? What made it clandestine? Time and place and circumstances?

- "Challenges had always been a part of my existence. The thrill of overcoming adversaries had fueled my existence for centuries..."

  Sounds great but how about showing us some of the challenges? Even more so, we would love to be shown the overcoming of specific adversaries, who they were and how and where it happened.

- "My thirst for learning now encompassed the wonders of science, bridging the gap between the ages past and the possibilities of the future."

How about showing us what you did for your learning to encompass the wonders of science? Show us how your "thirst" bridged the gap between the past and the future (!).

It is repetitive: The 650 words provide a very limited space to showcase all the salient qualities that make you a formidable candidate for admission into the college you have set your sights on. Do not waste any of your words by repeating what had already been explicitly stated or implicitly addressed.

For Example:

"a clandestine encounter with Dr. Van Helsing's blood transfusion attempt to save Lucy Westenra's life unveiled the astonishing possibilities of science"

And

"The sight of Dr. Van Helsing's blood transfusion apparatus, particularly Blundell's invention, was unlike anything I had ever seen."

And

"Dr. Van Helsing's mastery over this medical procedure was awe-inspiring. As I watched him navigate the complexities of Blundell's apparatus with precision…"

And

"The surreptitious witnessing of Dr. Van Helsing's blood transfusion endeavor marked a pivotal moment in my existence as Count Dracula."

And

"…the elixir of enlightenment that Dr. Van Helsing's experiment had bestowed upon me."

We got the point the first time: watching Dr. Van Helsing use an apparatus for blood transfusion was a pivotal moment. So, hey Chat Gpt, why did you repeat the same idea four more times given the very limited and limiting constraint of 650 words? Needless repetition is fluff and will only serve to hurt your chances of making a memorable impression on the college admissions officer.

The tone/persona is grandiose: While one must toot one's horn, one must do so in as unobtrusive manner as possible. The College Essay is the only real opportunity for the admissions committee to hear your voice and get a sense of your personality. Only by sounding like yourself—and not sounding like a generic high school senior applying for college—will you be able to make a memorable impression. But there is a caveat: you also must sound like someone the admissions committee would like to have on their college campus. So best to avoid a tone that makes you sound either arrogant or grandiose or simply too full of yourself! For example:

"As Count Dracula, the immortal embodiment of darkness"... "I have amassed a vast reservoir of knowledge"... "My understanding of life and death expanded, and I found myself pondering..."... "As Count Dracula, I now stood at the precipice of a new era."

Tone it down a little. Some humility, perhaps?!

The conclusion is repetitive: In a 650 word essay, you don't really have the luxury to write the type of repetitive conclusion taught in middle school 5-paragraph essays: repeat your central thesis to reinforce your argument. The last two paragraphs are redundant, especially the penultimate one that begins with the phrase, "In conclusion…"

In fact, consider the statement in the same paragraph: "The themes of learning, mastery, and challenge were intricately woven into this transformative experience." This statement commits two sins: that of repetition and of assuming a weak reader. The college admissions officer is a savvy reader. They get it. Chat Gpt's essay very clearly engages the thematic topics of learning, mastery, and challenge throughout the piece.

By repeating this in the conclusion, it shows lack of faith in either the reader or in the writing itself. And, as must be clear by now, Chat Gpt's essay is weak on many levels, so the cover up—a repetitive conclusion—is almost inevitable!

Finally, it exceeds the word limit by more than 100 words.

Gemini AI in Action

Vital Theme: LEARNING, also: mastery, challenge

Action that shows how theme is vital in Dracula's life: Seeing the blood transfusion in Lucy Westenra's case opened up Dracula's eyes to the possibilities of science in blood related matters

What object/person is memorable in that action: Blundell's blood transfusion apparatus that Dr. Van Helsing used to try to save Lucy

So, let us shape the above data into A PROMPT for GEMINI AI:

Hey GEMINI AI: Write a college essay of 650 words from the viewpoint of Count Dracula where he discusses how surreptitiously witnessing the blood transfusion Dr. Van Helsing conducted in order to try to save Lucy Westenra's life opened up his eyes to the possibilities of science, especially because he's seeing Blundell's blood transfusion apparatus for the first time. Please embed the themes of learning, mastery, and challenge.

Gemini AI's essay:

A Night of Discovery in Whitechapel by Gemini AI

Centuries of existence have instilled in me a certain cynicism. Innovation, progress — these were mere whispers in the grand tapestry of time. Yet, on a damp London night, shrouded in the fog of Whitechapel, I witnessed something that sent a tremor through the very core of my immortal being: a spark of human ingenuity that rivaled the brilliance of the alchemists of old.

My purpose that night was far less noble. Curiosity, a rare guest in my ancient halls, had been piqued by the frantic movements of the vampire hunters gathered around poor Lucy Westenra. Driven by a morbid fascination with their crusade, I found myself perched on a gargoyle overlooking the scene. What unfolded before me, however, transcended my initial morbid intent.

Dr. Van Helsing, the dogged leader of this human resistance, bustled around a contraption I had never encountered. It was a marvel of polished brass and glass tubes, shimmering with an almost otherworldly luminescence. Later, through whispers in the night, I learned of its purpose: a blood transfusion apparatus, a creation of a Dr. Blundell. The concept itself sent a jolt through me.

For centuries, my existence had revolved around one singular pursuit — the sustenance I derived from the vital essence of lifeblood. My methods, however crudely effective, were barbaric at best. Here, however, was a method — a calculated, almost elegant process — that sought to achieve the same end but with a finesse I never thought possible.

The flickering gaslight illuminated the scene as Dr. Van Helsing, with a surgeon's precision, meticulously connected the apparatus. The men around him, their faces etched with concern, watched with rapt attention. The tension crackled in the air, mirroring the electricity pulsing through the strange contraption.

Then, the blood flowed. A crimson river, stolen from the veins of one, offered as a lifeline to another. I watched, mesmerized, as the science unfolded. The sight of the life force, once my sole domain, being harnessed and manipulated in such a controlled manner ignited a curiosity that had long lain dormant.

The following days were a blur of focused observation. I haunted the shadows, a silent observer as the humans desperately fought to save Lucy. I devoured snippets of conversations, learning the principles behind blood types, the delicate balance required in the transfusion process, the very intricacies of the human circulatory system.

This nocturnal education was a revelation. The world, stagnant for so long in my eyes, suddenly teemed with the potential for discovery. This wasn't mere alchemy — this was science, a systematic approach to understanding the very essence of life.

Of course, the challenge of adapting this knowledge was immense. My very existence defied the laws of human biology. Could such techniques be applied to a being like me? The answer remained a tantalizing mystery.

However, the seed was sown. The thirst for knowledge, long dormant, bloomed within me. My focus shifted from merely acquiring sustenance to a deeper understanding of the very life force I depended on. I began scouring ancient libraries, devouring forgotten texts on medicine, anatomy, and the nascent field of biology.

The path of self-mastery took on a new dimension. It was no longer just about honing my vampiric abilities but about wrestling with this burgeoning scientific understanding. It was a pursuit fraught with frustration, the boundaries of my existence pushing back against every attempt to integrate this new knowledge.

Yet, the very challenge fueled me. With each hurdle overcome, with each obscure medical text deciphered, a sense of accomplishment bloomed within me. This was a different kind of thirst, as intoxicating as the richest blood, a thirst for knowledge that burned ever brighter.

The memory of that night in Whitechapel remains a turning point in my existence. It was a testament to the enduring human spirit, their unwavering pursuit of knowledge, and their willingness to challenge accepted limitations. It is a pursuit I now share, albeit from the shadows, forever a student in this grand experiment called life.

Merits:

Variety of sentence structure: Gemini AI is equally adept as Chat Gpt at varying sentence structure. Consider a sampling:

Em-dash: "Innovation, progress — these were mere whispers in the grand tapestry of time."

Appositive: "Curiosity, *a rare guest in my ancient halls*, had been piqued by the frantic movements of the vampire hunters…"

Rule of 3s: "It was a testament to the enduring human spirit, their unwavering pursuit of knowledge, and their willingness to challenge accepted limitations."

Short sentence (for dramatic effect): "The concept itself sent a jolt through me."

Adverbial modifier in a simple sentence: "The sight of the life force, once my sole domain, *being harnessed and manipulated in such a controlled manner* ignited a curiosity that had long lain dormant."

Note: As compared to Chat Gpt, Gemini AI avoids complex and compound sentence construction, relying instead on simple sentences loaded with modifying phrases and clauses.

Appropriate vocabulary: the word choice or diction suits the message being conveyed. The words are employed in their correct connotations and fit seamlessly with the message being conveyed. Reading this, we feel that the writer is using words they are familiar with and not reaching for thesaurus in order to impress.

- Cynicism
- Ingenuity
- Morbid
- Crusade
- Transcended
- Contraption
- Luminescence
- Sustenance
- Finesse
- Revelation
- Tantalizing
- Nascent
- Burgeoning

Figurative Language: metaphors, similes, imagery and the like are always welcome in fluid prose as they add a depth to the message by highlighting comparison & contrast, anchoring abstraction in concrete details.

- In the grand tapestry of time
- The tension crackled in the air
- I devoured snippets of conversation
- Sent a jolt through me
- The seed was sown

Imagery (the use of the five senses): "Yet, on a damp London night, shrouded in the fog of Whitechapel, I witnessed something that sent a tremor through the very core of my immortal being: a spark…"

Personification: "Curiosity, a rare guest in my ancient halls, had been piqued by the frantic movements of the vampire hunters…"

Alliteration: "certain cynicism," "fraught with frustration," "burned ever brighter."

Shortcomings:

The use of mixed metaphor: while metaphors are useful to enhancing the reading experience and giving concrete image to abstractions and concepts, the use of mixed metaphors is sloppy (if not the cause of a chuckle or two):

- "Innovation, progress — these were mere whispers in the grand tapestry of time." (how can whispers be spoken in a tapestry?)
- "A crimson river, stolen from the veins of one, offered as a lifeline to another." (how can a river also be a lifeline?)
- "The thirst for knowledge…bloomed within me." (how can thirst also be a flower?)

Lack of details/specifics: Here again, I must remind you that the devil (of any task) is in the details. The details provided in the Gemini AI essay remain at the level of generalities. There are many missed opportunities where specifics could have been provided and would have gone a long way into legitimizing the validity of the experience and its impact on shaping the applicant's academic interests. For example:

- *"I began scouring ancient libraries, devouring forgotten texts on medicine, anatomy, and the nascent field of biology."*

This is vague and too general for the purpose of the college essay. Which texts? What titles? Be specific, Gemini!

- *"It was no longer just about honing my vampiric abilities but about wrestling with this burgeoning scientific understanding."*

What vampiric abilities? What are some details of this new scientific understanding?

- *"It was a pursuit fraught with frustration, the boundaries of my existence pushing back against every attempt to integrate this new knowledge."*

Again, here it would be very useful for the purpose of persuading an admissions officer if Gemini gave specific details of this new knowledge.

- *"Yet, the very challenge fueled me. With each hurdle overcome, with each obscure medical text deciphered, a sense of accomplishment bloomed within me."*

Sounds good, but what are some titles of these obscure medical texts, and what are some specific details that were deciphered? Eh, Gemini, eh?

Errors in factual details: AI is known to hallucinate, fabricate, and obfuscate. In this essay, Gemini AI gets a couple of crucial facts very wrong:

- *"A Night of Discovery in Whitechapel"*

The title gets the location wrong! Whitechapel is the impoverished neighborhood associated with Jack the Ripper. The events discussed in the essay occur at Hillingham, Lucy Westenra's residence, located in the well to do neighborhood of Hampstead.

- *"I devoured snippets of conversations, learning the principles behind blood types, the delicate balance required in the transfusion process, the very intricacies of the human circulatory system."*

The principles behind blood types were unknown during Van Helsing's time; in fact, it is one of the amusing facts that Lucy is saved through what science would consider blind luck since none of the donors knew if their blood types matched Lucy's (or that there was such a thing as blood type!).

Verdict on the use of AI for help on writing
The College Essay

If you've read the the two previous samplings from Chat Gpt and Gemini AI and read the detailed critique of the merits and shortcomings of the writing, then the takeaways are clear:

The Good Side of AI

- AI employs vocabulary that is appropriate.
- AI employs varied sentence structures to create effective rhythm.
- AI uses figurative language to enrich the context.
- AI can be prompted to create an essay with a thematic focus.
- AI is grammatically sound.

The Bad Side of AI

- AI is repetitive.
- AI is vague.
- AI uses figurative language awkwardly (example: mixed metaphors).
- AI gets its factual details wrong.
- AI does not have specific details of your life!

How do I use AI as a helper?

- Do the worksheets in as much detail as you can.
- Make sure you cross-reference your thematic topics in worksheet 2 with those lurking in your responses in Worksheet 1.
- Spend time fleshing out as many details (I cannot say it enough: the devil is in the details) as possible.
- Write Narratives for at least three entries (preferably five) in Worksheet 4.
- Create very specific prompts that use thematic topics + specific details from worksheet 1 and 3 for AI to generate drafts.
- Read the drafts with a critical eye.
- Use the information to write your very own, very "Memorable Me"!

CHAPTER 12
Dracula's Gems (Rewritten College Essays)

Prompt 7. Share an essay on any topic of your choice. It can be one you have already written, one that responds to a different prompt, or one of your own design.

A Kaleidoscope of Difference by Count Dracula

I hovered unnoticed outside Lucy Westenra's window. Inside, two men helped an unknown third unpack unfamiliar instruments from a wooden case. They were variously brass and silver colored: a funnel, a couple of thin, curved and tapering pipes, a rod, and a formidable looking syringe. There was a flurry of activity. The stranger directed Dr. Seward, the head of the lunatic asylum, and Holmwood, Lucy's fiancé, to assemble the pieces into a novel contraption. My curiosity turned to amazement as they inserted the tapering end of one silver pipe into a vein in Lucy's arm; the other into a similar vein in Holmwood's arm. What infernal device was this? What were they doing to my poor, beloved Lucy? Judging by her gaunt face, sunken eyes and lifeless cheeks, she was but a slumber or two away from crossing over to the undead state of being and becoming my forever bride.

And yet, just as I was about to crash through the window and effect a gallant rescue, I noticed something miraculous—her pallor became suffused with a rosy flush and soon enough, life and color had returned to her face. The transformation was uncanny. There was only one explanation—these gentlemen had re-blooded my Lucy. The apparatus had managed some sort of transfusion of blood.

Through the ages, I had perfected the art of painlessly draining blood, but these gentlemen had engineered the reverse using Blundell's innovative apparatus.

From this moment forward, I became passionate about science—its experiments, its possibilities, its discoveries.

I applied to become a laboratory assistant in the Department of Pathological Anatomy at the University of Vienna. Working under Karl Landsteiner, I assisted in research in the field of morbid physiology and pathological anatomy. Aiding and observing the work of a group of tireless scientific pioneers, I felt exhilarated as they discovered new facts about immunological factors in syphilis, paroxysmal haemoglobinuria, and poliomyelitis. But my greatest joy was being present when Prof. Landsteiner's meticulous and systematic investigations into blood transfusions resulted in his classifying blood types as A, B, AB, and O. It was in Vienna, too, that Landsteiner's lab launched the investigation into bleeding in the newborn; and although the discovery of Rh-factors in blood was documented by him in New York a couple of decades later, I kept close correspondence and felt equally elated as part of his team at the Rockefeller Institute for Medical Research.

While I am still fascinated by research into the chemistry of antigens, antibodies, and other immunological occurrences in human blood, the proliferation of scientific knowledge in genetics has whetted my appetite in many other directions. I would love to study the relevance of Mendelian inheritance in quantitative genetics, the gain of function in dominant negative alleles, as well as the genetic variance in response to environmental factors through haplotype mapping.

Even more exciting are the possibilities created by the overlap of once distinct scientific fields. Does genetic research fall under the domain of biology, chemistry, biochemistry, biophysics, data analytics, combinatorics, or even algorithms & programming?

I am excited to enroll in your college and gain exposure by taking courses in various departments. I would love to converse with professors about their research and would cherish the opportunity to participate in as many research teams as possible. I am equally looking forward to socializing on campus with similarly motivated peers.

My quest for knowledge is fueled by the desire to know more about not only what makes us different but also what makes us the same. In genetic terms, we are all 99.5% identical. That 0.5% difference, however, is what populates the world with a panorama of diversity and a kaleidoscope of difference. In learning about us, I will also learn about me. And the more I know about where I come from, the better I will be able to map out the journey of where I must go.

(Word Count 648)

Prompt 7. Share an essay on any topic of your choice. It can be one you have already written, one that responds to a different prompt, or one of your own design.

Unseen Reflection by Count Dracula

My bare feet slapped the cobblestones as I bolted through the Istanbul bazaar, thankful for the cacophony of shouts and bartering that drowned out my ragged breaths. I weaved between towering displays of ceramics and piles of fabric, finding refuge behind a rack of embroidered caftans. A glint of gold amidst the silks caught my eye, and I couldn't resist looking into the handheld mirror, its etched frame cool against trembling fingers. It was then, as a terrified three year old trying to calm my hammering heart and ragged breathing that I first discovered I was different: in the mirror I saw no reflection of myself.

The world knows me as the vampire with the tall stature, the aristocratic features, and the piercing eyes, and I have to take the world at its word. For since that day I have been trying to dispel the hollowness in my chest upon seeing a chilling absence where my face should have been.

As I grew into my current state, this anomaly created a thirst for knowledge that I am in pursuit of till this day. It took three long centuries before the scientific spirit infusing the human race could provide me even an inkling into the peculiar nature of my existence. It was in Dr. Walter Flemming's cytology lab in 1882 that we witnessed a powerful revelation under the lens of his light microscope as I observed the dance of chromosomes in my blood. Among the x and y, an extra chromosome.

I was neither xx (female) nor xy (male), but xxy (me).

This discovery resonated with the hollowness of the unseen reflection. Was it this chromosomal aberration that set me apart from the very beings I sustained myself upon? I immersed myself in countless hours of research of chromatin formation during mitosis, and saw my nails permanently blackened by the aniline dye used to stain salamander embryos, yet never reached any definitive results.

Years turned into decades, the world convulsed in bloody wars, but my quest for understanding continued unabated. In the 1940s, I found myself face-to-face with Dr. Harry Klinefelter, the man who unwittingly labeled my preexisting condition by his name, the Klinefelter Syndrome.

When I explained to him the absence of a reflection, the extra chromosome in my nucleus, and the uniqueness of my vampirical form, Dr. Klinefelter was awestruck and offered me full access to his research and resources.

It was a moment of unprecedented collaboration that I cherish to this day. Instead of the habitual dynamic of hunter and hunted, Klinefelter and I became partners grappling with the anomaly that resided within me. We were united by the pursuit of discovery, a shared thirst for understanding the unseen threads that weave together the fabric of existence in the universe. Our initial findings proved that the condition was not inherited, its abnormalities were not predictable, and its cure was not essential.

The journey that began with a missing reflection has become an odyssey of self-discovery. I am a creature of duality — and most see me as a monster who exists outside the human web of affairs yet forever tethered to it like a parasite. I am of the belief, however, that we are united in sharing identical C, T, A and Gs and differ only in their encoded blueprints. And within the framework of evolution, who is to say that my blueprint might not be a step in the right direction in humanity's evolutionary march through time?

I, Count Dracula, am much misunderstood. My uniqueness is both a burden and a blessing, a constant reminder that the world holds more secrets than any moonlight can reveal. The pursuit of knowledge, however, offers a flicker of hope, a path towards understanding the unseen thread that binds me to existence, even in the absence of my reflection.

(word count 637)

Prompt 2. The lessons we take from obstacles we encounter can be fundamental to later success. Recount a time when you faced a challenge, setback, or failure. How did it affect you, and what did you learn from the experience?

(A revised version of Dracula's original essay for prompt 2)

Chess not Checkers by Count Dracula

From the campaigns I waged over the centuries—as King and Commander in the Dark Ages, as Count and C.E.O in the Modern Ages—the setback that makes me most rueful is an episode in England, in 1899. There, I identified a woman worthy of ascension to Queen of the Vampires: Mina Harker.

My first glimpse of Mina, and I realized why London had been calling me all along, why I had endured passage in choppy seas, and why I had acquired properties all across that grimy city. Here she was, kin of my kin, yearning for the liberation that only my incision on the hollow of her neck could deliver.

But to transform Mina into becoming the queen of my coterie of undead countesses proved to be a failure.

My objectives were constantly thwarted by Dr. Van Helsing, the canniest adversary to ever have crossed my path and survived. At me he thrust garlic, at me he brandished the Cross, at me he tossed sacramental wafers—never knowing it was the allergens they contained that repelled me!

The Helsing gang burst upon me during that primal moment when I had Mina entranced, ensconced in my bosom, and suckling the very life blood from the freshly incised artery in my chest. Mina had succumbed, her barriers had dissipated, and she was moments from merging. Perhaps I fell prey to my own overconfidence, but I failed to hear them until it was too late.

To my dismay, they were armed with all of the aforementioned allergens that debilitate me. I was forced to exit. At the time, I was rather sanguine about finding Mina to complete our vampirical baptism.

How wrong was I!

They worked in concert to infiltrate and booby trap all my coffin-boxes around London—in Carfax, Bermondsey, Mile End, Walworth. They ambushed me at my abode in Piccadilly. I was chased out of London and stalked all the way to my home in Transylvania. And Mina, I was never able to deliver the poor soul from her mortal existence.

This failure affected me deeply. Despite my superior being, I was thwarted by mere mortals.

After much reflection, I realized that my enterprise suffered from inadequate preparation, planning, and execution in three domains: delegation, anticipation, and underestimation.

Delegation. I cannot be at multiple places at once. When faced by an enemy united in their numbers and coordinated in their actions, I cannot outmaneuver them by myself. For my expedition to London, I should have conscripted the services of the Three Sisters instead of leaving them behind to toy with Jonathan Harker. I should have used that profligate lunatic Renfield to greater advantage instead of too soon ending his misery.

Anticipation. Sure, I was strategic in my plans, from the purchase of properties in prime locations, to shipping more than adequate supplies of native-soil coffins, to preying on my chosen ones at the most opportune times. However, I paid scant regard to the possibility that my human foes were equally endowed with strategic acumen. While they anticipated my every move, I failed to examine their countermoves—they were playing chess not checkers. It was a humbling realization.

Underestimation: I was too quick to peg the Helsing gang with the fanatics I had encountered for centuries, people wed to superstition and dying for divine intervention. But Helsing's swiftness for scientific experimentation was instrumental in defeating me. They figured out that the soil in my coffin had nutrients essential to my regeneration. They almost saved Lucy by administering blood transfusions. They collated records of their interactions with me in order to analyze my predatory habits and create plans based on hard logic. They exploited my telepathic bond with Mina. Underestimating their scientific acumen cost me victory.

Moving forward, I resolved to essentialize teamwork in any enterprise, evaluate all possible outcomes before taking action, and respect the competition as I would wish to be respected myself.

(word count 650)

Describe a topic, idea, or concept you find so engaging that it makes you lose all track of time. Why does it captivate you? What or who do you turn to when you want to learn more?

(A revised version of Dracula's original essay for prompt 6)

The Creation of Wonder by Count Dracula

Mastery.

The gift of time allowed me to conceive all of my actions in pursuit of becoming a master—of skill, of craft, and of accomplishment. In my heart of hearts, the forms of mastery I have pursued have had one goal: how to pull humanity out of their lives of self-inflicted violence and suffering, and how to instill in them a likeness of my being.

Becoming the Master is an infinitely consuming task. When time stretches out like an endless scroll, it becomes easy, much too easy, to lose one's bearings. In my life as a Boyar, I became master to the Peasants and also the Szigane; yet I would be remiss if I didn't share the fact that I spent a couple of centuries achieving what could have taken decades, but perfection takes time, and I was their perfect master.

Though my misfortunate foray into England more than a century ago could be considered a failure, it did not lack effort in mastery. Prior to orchestrating the arrival of Jonathan Harker to my castle in Transylvania, I had lost myself for decades in the study of everything British. I had mastered the language, the customs, and the idioms. Each and every book on the subject of England that I could lay my hands on, had I devoured. Each and every guest hailing from the British Isles, had I absorbed for cultural cues. Yet the second I greeted Jonathan, it became obvious that still I lacked the intonation of an Englishman. I knew the grammar and the vocabulary, but I knew not the language they spoke. So I redoubled my efforts to absorb everything Jonathan had to offer.

And even though England didn't work out the way I had hoped, not once did anyone there suspect I was anything other than a proper Englishman going about his business in the crowded streets of mighty London, in the midst of the whirl and rush of humanity.

To be a master of all and servant to none requires a painstaking commitment to continuous learning. Through the centuries, I have always gravitated to the centers of civilization with a view to mastering the essential knowledge that makes each civilization dominant in its era. In ancient Greece, you could find me in the shadows of the marketplace in the Acropolis, lending a keen year to the Sophistic argumentation between Protagoras and Diogenes. In Mauryan India, I partook with King Ashoka in both the massacre at Kalinga as well as in his ensuing adoption of Buddhist tenets. How often, in the Roman Colosseum, did I smuggle in myself as a gladiator to perfect my combat skills with the large-shielded but single greaved scutarius and double-greaved parmularius. When the Yong Le Emperor decreed that the Great Wall be built in China, I immersed myself with the engineers to perfect the masonry that enabled the creation of that seventh wonder of the world.

Which brings me to the United States, the wonder of the modern world, the Mecca of exponentially proliferating knowledge, invention, and innovation. So diverse are the options for the pursuit of mastery that my immersion in all things American will be my longest in any culture, past or present.

I am in a delirium of anticipation as I consider what majors to explore in college first: shall I learn the psychotropic details of tetrahydrocannabinol in the Chemistry major, or develop virtual cognition in the Video Gaming major, or inspect evidence from organismal and ecological perspectives in the Forensics major? Or, better yet, shall I profit from American expediency and triple-major all at once?

I will be a kid in a candy shop on the college campus, reaching for a taste and a nibble of a range of subjects and electives, before I sink my teeth in to specialize in a major and master the subjects of my choosing.

(world count 648)

APPENDIX
The Memorable Me Worksheets

Step 1: MEMORABLE ME—The Questionnaire

So. Let's get this show on the road.

We are going to begin with a series of questions that are designed to help you take a deep dive into who you are to discover some of the things that make you You.

Think of this as: What makes me authentic? What makes me me?

As you answer these questions, think carefully and be truthful.

We are looking for your Memorable Me, and we won't discover it if you are being either evasive or flippant about the answer to these questions.

By the way, most of these questions go back around 150 years—back in the day when there were no distractions such as video gaming, ipads, social media, on demand streaming and binge watching shows.

People had time on their hands, and they'd answer these types of questions for fun.

So, have fun with it. Do as Marcel Proust did and discover your inner hero!

1. What is your current state of mind?

2. What is your idea of happiness?

3. Who makes you laugh more than anyone?

4. What do you consider your greatest achievement?

5. Best gift you ever received?

6. What is your most treasured possession?

7. Which person past or present do you most admire?

8. Your favorite occupation when you're not working?

9. If you could change one thing about yourself, what would it be?

10. What do you most value in your friends?

11. If not yourself, who would you be?

12. If you had a clone, what would you have it do?

13. What is your pet peeve?

14. When and where are you happiest?

15. What talent would you most like to have?

16. What is your greatest extravagance?

17. What is the trait you most deplore in yourself?

18. Your idea of misery?

19. What is your greatest fear?

20. What can you do better?

21. Who broke your heart?

22. What is the trait you most deplore in others?

23. What is your greatest regret?

24. What do you tolerate the least?

25. What is your favorite painting?

26. Three words that describe you?

27. Three words others use to describe you?

28. What are you listening to?

29. On what occasion do you lie?

30. What do you consider the most overrated virtue?

Step 2: Discovering My Vital Themes

You are the hero of the story of your life, "My Journey So Far." Cue in your favorite English class here: "every story has themes that are vital to its message."

What are the thematic topics that excite you, motivate you, drive you?

What have you come to believe strongly in? What is of fundamental importance to the hero that you are becoming in your "Journey So Far"?

1. Circle as many Vital Themes below that resonate with you.

Abundance	Diversity	Learning	Resourcefulness
Acceptance	Empathy	Love	Responsibility
Achievement	Encouragement	Loyalty	Responsiveness
Adaptability	Enthusiasm	Making a difference	Security
Advancement	Ethics	Mindfulness	Self-Control
Adventure	Excellence	Motivation	Selflessness
Advocacy	Expressiveness	Optimism	Simplicity
Ambition	Fairness	Open-mindedness	Stability
Appreciation	Family	Originality	Success
Autonomy	Fashion	Performance	Teamwork
Balance	Friendship	Personal development	Thoughtfulness
Being the Best	Flexibility	Proactive	Traditionalism
Benevolence	Freedom	Professionalism	Trustworthiness
Boldness	Fun	Quality	Understanding
Brilliance	Generosity	Recognition	Uniqueness
Calmness	Gratitude	Risk-taking	Usefulness
Caring	Grace	Safety	Versatility
Challenge	Growth	Service	Vision
Charity	Harmony	Spirituality	Warmth
Cheerfulness	Happiness	Stability	Wealth
Cleverness	Health	Perfection	Well-Being
Community	Humility	Peace	Wisdom
Commitment	Humor	Playfulness	Zeal
Compassion	Inclusiveness	Popularity	(add your own below)
Cooperation	Interdependence	Power	
Collaboration	Individuality	Preparedness	
Consistency	Innovation	Proactivity	
Contribution	Inquiry	Professionalism	
Creativity	Inspiration	Punctuality	
Curiosity	Intelligence	Recognition	
Daring	Intuition	Relationships	
Decisiveness	Joy	Reliability	
Dedication	Kindness	Resilience	
Dependability	Knowledge		
	Leadership		

2. Copy down all the Vital Themes you circled:

3. Narrow it down to your top 5 Vital Themes:

4. Pick your top three Vital Themes and copy them down in the box below:

My Vital Themes

1.	2.	3.

5. Crosscheck: Take your Vital Themes and cross-reference them with your responses in the "Getting to Know Myself" worksheet.

Are the Vital Themes reflected in the responses from worksheet #1?

Yes	No
Congratulations! You have your Vital Themes.	Go back to Step 1 above (and be truthful)

You can now begin crafting the story of "My Journey So Far"!

Step 3: My Vital Themes in Action

From the My Vital Themes exercise you did on the worksheet, enter the top three to five in the first column.

Then, in the second column, jot down an action/experience/encounter that shows how the theme is vital to your life. It could be something in the past, something in the present, or even something you foresee in the future.

Finally, in the third column, anchor the action onto an object/person that is key to the experience.

Vital Themes Ranked in order of importance	What is an action that shows how my theme is vital in my life?	What is an object/person that is memorable in that action?
1.		
2.		
3.		
4.		
5.		

Step 4: Launch "My Journey So Far"

Now, take one item from your box in Step 3 and write out the short story behind it: why is it so vital to who you are? What happened to make it vital? Who was involved? Where and when did the story take place? What insight did you gain?

Tip #1: Show! This means using vivid description, engaging the five senses: touch, taste, sight, sound, and smell.

Tip #2: Look at the work you did in choosing the worksheets My Vital Themes and Vital Themes in Action. Use these Vital Themes and Vital Actions if you can in telling your story.

Tip #3: Don't worry about the length/word count of your story (we will deal with that later!).

Tip #4: Give your story a title. But, do this only AFTER you have written out your story.

Special Item:

Title:

Story:

Step 5: Draft of "My Journey So Far"

Great news; in the previous worksheet, you already launched your story of your journey so far. This means that you already have a great hook and something original because it tells us what makes you the hero of your own life, a hero with a compelling story to share.

Now, your task is to complete the draft. Cut and paste your launch story. Then, transition from your launch story into any of the cardinal components listed below to complete your draft.

1. What you have experienced in life (most likely, already in your launch story)

2. What you have done in life (might already be in your launch story)

3. Who you are today (add details of key academic & extracurricular pursuits)

4. What you want to do in the future (what are your aspirations?)

5. Who you will become tomorrow (need not be explicit; step 1-4 convey this)

Title of your story:

(story of "My Journey So Far" ~650 words)